D1606680

BIRTH ORDER AND LIFE ROLES

BIRTH ORDER AND LIFE ROLES

By

LUCILLE K. FORER, Ph.D.

C H A R L E S   C   T H O M A S   •   P U B L I S H E R
Springfield • Illinois • U.S.A.

Published and Distributed Throughout the World by
CHARLES C THOMAS • PUBLISHER
BANNERSTONE HOUSE
301-327 East Lawrence Avenue, Springfield, Illinois, U.S.A.
NATCHEZ PLANTATION HOUSE
735 North Atlantic Boulevard, Fort Lauderdale, Florida, U.S.A.

With THOMAS BOOKS *careful attention is given to all details of
manufacturing and design. It is the Publisher's desire to present books
that are satisfactory as to their physical qualities and artistic possibilities
and appropriate for their particular use.* THOMAS BOOKS *will be true
to those laws of quality that assure a good name and good will.*

Printed in the United States of America

To Those Who Gave Me My Place in the Family:

My Mother and My Father, Jo Ann and William
My Sister, Bette
My Brothers, Ken and Roland

INTRODUCTION

I WAS the first child of my parents. I was followed by a brother and a sister and then, after a long period of time, by another brother. While these facts were not of great importance to the world in general, they seemed very important to me.

The sequence of events meant that I held the position in the family of *oldest* child. For some reason that might have to do with the fact that I later became a clinical psychologist. I experienced my role as oldest child with considerable conscious recognition of what it meant to be in that place in the family. As oldest child I had many advantages. It was always my place to head up the sibling line in the family whether it was for the largest number of cookies or to have the first sight of the annual Christmas tree. Being oldest was a source of much pride and with it went a feeling of strength.

But there were also disadvantages which became more apparent as I grew older. Being oldest meant more responsibility relative to the other children at any one time. Of great significance to me was the feeling that I was, as my mother said, a "guinea pig" for my parents in raising children. It seemed to me that I was perpetually striving with my parents over matters that the younger children in the family would find already solved by me when it came their turn to want greater freedom, more adult clothes, or whatever the subject of struggle was between adolescent and parent.

When I became an adult, it seemed to me that I could perceive a continuation of many childhood attitudes and behavioral tendencies which had first appeared in my relationship with my two brothers and sister and my parents in my place as oldest child. I felt that these attitudes came into play in my relationships with my other adult friends. It seemed even more apparent to me that they influenced my relationship with my husband and later with my children.

I was not the first person, of course, to wonder if the sibling place in the family might not have an important part in the development of human beings. The first statistical evidence presented in print seems to have been that of Sir Francis Galton who, in 1874, said he had found that eminent male scientists were far more likely to be first children in their families than later children.[1] Many following studies were made particularly by persons in the field of education who hoped to find relationships between the learning or school behavior problems of children and their places in the family as only child, oldest child, middle, or youngest child.

As a student of psychology I learned how contradictory and inconclusive the results of these studies were considered to be by the savants in the field.

However my interest in the matter continued. While teaching a college class in adolescent psychology, I decided to make an informal search of the psychological literature for studies of sibling relationships to see if I could find any confirmation of some of my hypotheses concerning the effect of growing up in a certain family place.

I was delighted to find evidence for some consistent differences, especially between first-born and later-born children. First-born children, who include both only children and children with younger siblings, were found to tend toward more easily aroused anger than were later-born children. First-born children who had younger siblings were consistently revealed to be more likely to display jealousy than were only children who had no siblings.

The findings were sparse, but they were encouraging. These two results were in line with psychoanalytic theories about the development of personality. Who but the first-born child could be expected to be tense and angry with parental pressures constantly on him as he grew up? Who but the oldest child could be expected to be jealous? Had not younger brothers and sisters moved in to take his place with his parents and to share his possessions? It was of special interest that the only child, also a first-born, tended not to display jealousy to any great degree. The only child, of course, is not subject to competition from siblings. It seemed to me that these findings gave some support to the possibility that the position of the individual in the childhood family might be of great importance in determining some of the child and adult characteristics of that person.

As I continued in my practice as a clinical psychologist, I found the people with whom I worked presenting me with what seemed to be increasingly clear evidence of the effect on them of having been raised in a certain place in the family.

Persons raised in certain family positions repeatedly described the same effects coming out of each of those positions. As they became more conscious of those effects, they often reacted with an insightful, "But of course!"

Best of all, the increased self-understanding seemed relatively easily followed by a change in attitudes and behavior which improved their relationships with other people. To take just one example, a man was able recently to so reorganize his perception of himself as a youngest child trying to be a responsible husband, that he changed his behavior and saved a very shaky marriage. This case of "psychotherapy" required one hour of discussion between therapist and patient.

My clinical observations of the effect of sibling relationships have not been limited to those involving persons with whom I have worked in a professional capacity. I have gathered information from the majority of persons with whom I have come in contact. These have included students, colleagues, other members of community and social groups to which I belong, my children and their friends, my own siblings and their family members. As my friends know, I have been unceasingly aggressive in questioning them about their relationships with brothers and sisters, and I hope they know how much I have appreciated their patience with me. My justification, if there is one, for this prying behavior is that most people seem to welcome the opportunity to talk about their sibling relationships.

Through the years, in addition to my own observation and study, I have also benefited from the interest and wise communications of my husband, Dr. Bertram R. Forer, concerning what he has seen of the influence of early sibling relationships and place in the family on many persons with whom he has come in contact as a clinical psychologist.

I continued to watch the literature for pertinent studies, and it has been my pleasure to see scientific attention change from great skepticism to an acceptance of family position as an authentic and provocative subject of serious experimental approaches. The number of studies increases greatly each succeeding year. I have in my files summaries of more than five hundred attempts to probe some aspect of the effect of sibling relationships on the development of the individual. The worldwide nature of the interest in the subject is shown by the fact that these studies have been made all around the globe: in India, small Guatemalan villages, Kaiwan, Scandinavia, and in the United States, to name a few locations. However, I have found few books devoted to the subject. As far as I know, this book is the first attempt to integrate much of the available research findings with impressions obtained in a clinical setting.

An interesting source of additional information for me has been that of autobiographies. These not only reveal childhood relationships with parents, brothers and sisters, but they offer us a means of seeing how these relationships might influence adult behavior, feelings, and attitudes of the writers.

As a result of having taken these multiple and varied approaches to the study of the effect of family position and having found many consistent results, I am able to present to you material in which I have considerable confidence. While the information must be considered preliminary in view of the tremendous amount of research still required, it will serve to direct your attention to what may be one of the most potent forces in shaping your life.

Since I have obtained information from many sources, I have been able to combine specific details in such a way that no one individual or family is described, except in the case of examples taken from published autobiographies. The names of such real persons are given in full. In the constructed examples, first names are usually used, but any name that is used is taken from the plays of Shakespeare.[2]

REFERENCES

1. GALTON, FRANCIS: *English Men of Science*. London, Macmillan, 1874.
2. SHAKESPEARE, WILLIAM: *Complete Works*. New York, Collier, 1925.

C**O**NTENTS

Contents

BIRTH ORDER AND LIFE ROLES

Chapter I

HOW YOUR BIRTH ORDER INFLUENCES YOUR LIFE ADJUSTMENT

WHEN we are born into a family unit or brought into it through adoption or as a step-child, we take a certain place in the family hierarchy. We become *only* child, *oldest* child, *middle* child, or *youngest* child.

The first and most obvious effect of taking a certain position in the family is the relationship we have with respect to the people already there. If there are only adults present, we are in a very close and often intense relationship with them, as anyone knows who has had a child or who has watched first-time parents hovering over their infants. This constant and close relationship gives the first child in the family an opportunity to imitate and learn from these adults to the fullest possible extent. The first child imitates their physical mannerisms and learns speech from them. He learns many more things and much of the learning takes place on an *unconscious* level. That is, neither the parents nor the child verbalize that thus and so is the way to do something. The child observes and imitates.

Our parents are the models for us in learning how to be human beings. And whether what they have to teach us is good or bad, comfortable or uncomfortable, learning from them starts us on our way toward becoming civilized people. This is a fact that is sometimes recognized with dismay by persons who have been dissatisfied with their parents. After criticizing them intensely, such persons are likely to have to accept the unwelcome recognition that they are much like those parents they have been criticizing.

Becoming a civilized human being involves a great deal more than learning how to walk and how to talk and how to handle a knife and fork at the table. It involves learning ways of relating to other people, incorporating the values and standards that make one fully a human being. Much of this basic learning takes place during our nursery years and while we are in a close relationship with our parents.

Usually we have two parents. They not only differ in sex but they differ in many other ways. Each of them has learned his or her own pattern of behavior, attitudes toward other people, values and standards which motivate them to feel and to act in certain ways. The first child in the family has two choices of imitation or identification in any one area. He can be like his father in one aspect, but like his mother in another. He tends to pick up more of the characteristics of the parent of the same sex, especially those patterns of behavior that have to do with physical action. A boy will tend to walk and move like his father and a girl to be like her mother in these characteristics. In emotional and other psychological characteristics, identification is more variable and complicated. In any event, identification is usually with characteristics of a parent if there are no other children in the family.

From the beginning the parents treat the child in accordance with his place in the family and soon the child recognizes that place. He is *the child* in the family, and he tends to think of himself as a child in relation to adults. The only child never has any reason to change such perception of his role and he tends to carry into adulthood a strong feeling of being a child in relation to other people.

The first child, who becomes the older or oldest child, does not have this unlimited time to view himself as the child in the relationship with his parents. When a sibling arrives, he tries to suppress the view of himself as a child and he struggles to be *parental*. We shall find that in both childhood and adulthood the older or oldest child's emphasis upon being "parental" offers him both advantages and problems.

Children who follow the first child in the family come into a situation where the relationship with the parent is, except in most unusual cases, shared with another child. The parents themselves have been changed by the preceding child or children in many ways. They are more experienced as parents. They may not welcome their later children with as much delight as they did their first child,[1] but they are probably less tense and anxious about being able to care for them properly. The later children enjoy many advantages as a result of having more relaxed parents. They benefit from the tendency of parents to try out ideas on their first child and to be more tolerant with later children. After testing judgments about matters ranging from when to toilet train a child to attitudes taken about dating, parents are relatively certain of approaches to take with later children and they are usually more relaxed (and exhausted) ones.

The first child serves as a barrier between later children and the parents. He is one of the models for his siblings. Later children in a family do not feel the same dependency on the parents for sustenance and companionship as did the first child. They have a "peer" to turn to when the parents are not available. Consequently they do not have such intense feelings of loneliness when the attention of the parents is directed elsewhere, nor do they seem to feel so inadequate when they do not meet the standards of their parents.

Extremely important in differentiating later children from first children is the extent to which direct identification with the parents is diluted for the later children. The later children seem more content to move gradually from child to adult. They do not seem to try as hard, as does the oldest child, to be parental and adult even during childhood.

These, then, are some of the differences in relationship with parents that result from having different places in the family hierarchy. Now let us look at some of the other areas of behavior which are affected by the child's order of birth in the family.

The child becomes known as the family's only child, oldest child, middle child, or youngest child, depending on his birth order. He is thought and talked about as having that place in the family. Both in his mind and in the minds of other people an important part of his identity is his family position.

The other members of the family assume certain attitudes toward each child in terms of his birth order. Parents usually expect their oldest child to be more capable and more responsible than the younger children. The oldest child comes to think about himself in the same way. These ways of seeing himself, of thinking about himself because of his sibling role become part of his self concept.

Older or oldest brother or sister tends to develop a self-concept that includes the belief that "I can do many things better than my siblings can. I am more adequate than other people in many situations."

The middle child comes to think of himself as sometimes better able to do things than other people because he is usually more capable than his younger sibling or siblings. Sometimes, though, he must turn to his older sibling or to his parents for help and so he comes to think of himself as able to obtain help when he needs it.

The youngest child tends to think, "I am less able to do many things than other people. But I need not be concerned because there are always others around to take care of me." This brings to mind a statement that former President Lyndon B. Johnson is reputed to have made about his two daughters. He was quoted as saying that he did not need to worry about either of the two girls because the older would always be able to take care of herself and the younger would always have someone around to take care of her.

The role we take as the result of being in a certain place in the family not only causes us to think about ourselves in certain ways, but it also causes us to think about other people in certain ways. The oldest tends to expect other people to be relatively less capable. The middle child has less specific expectations about the capabilities of other people. The youngest may see others as more adequate while the only child tends to think, "I am most secure when there are parents around to take care of me, but when they are not there, I have no one to turn to for help. So I'd better learn to take care of myself as much as possible."

The place in the family establishes for the child a specific role to be played within the family group. It influences him to develop certain attitudes toward himself and toward other people and helps him develop specific patterns of behavior.

The child also uses his role in the family to obtain status and recognition and as a basis for competing with the other members of the family in obtaining as much as possible of the good things that any family makes available to its members. Parents are usually relatively benevolent in their wish to distribute the resources of the family evenly among their children. Not so those peers, those siblings who are at the same relative level of becoming civilized.

Each child wants as much as he can obtain of the good things that are available from allowances to the time and attention of the parents.

The relative sizes and intellectual development of the children tend to establish the limits of their abilities in competing with each other. But human beings have many more ways of competing with each other than using physical size and strength. Each child in the family soon learns to use any possible aspects of his position to cope with his competitors.

The oldest child usually has the most natural position of supremacy, and he utilizes his advantages of strength and ability to take more responsibility in competing with his siblings. The frequent ploy of the youngest child is to turn his relative smallness and weakness to advantage. "Mommy," he complains, "Blanch never lets me win this game." Mother takes his older sister aside and says, "Why don't you let him win occasionally? You know it isn't any fun to play when you're always the loser.'" Or the younger or youngest child screams, "Mom! Henry is hitting me again!" And Mother scolds Henry, making the younger child feel protected and valued and that he has a most effective way of competing with big brother.

The middle child learns to use whatever position is of value at the moment, that of being bigger and stronger than the little ones or of being weaker than the older ones. The only child finds that emphasizing his role as "the child" with his parents is most successful in enlisting their protection and aid.

Thus the individual learns that he has a certain role in the family; that other people see him in certain ways in terms of that role. He tends to think of himself in those ways and he learns to behave in accordance with his role. He tends to think of other people in ways that accord with their status relative to his and he learns ways of using his own position that will enable him to compete successfully with his family rivals. Inevitably, he carries these attitudes toward himself and other people and his ways of relating to siblings into the world outside his home. He uses them first in friendship and school relationships in early childhood. By the time he is an adult they have become an integral part of his behavior.

He has learned to put certain aspects of his role to advantage and in adulthood he seeks ways of continuing the behavior found in childhood to be successful. He will, for instance, tend to select people to be with who will permit him to exercise the successful patterns of behavior. The oldest child usually has experienced satisfaction from his position of responsibility among his siblings. In adulthood he tends to select persons for close relationships who will permit him to continue having that satisfaction. He is likely to avoid selecting other oldest children to be his friends. Such unconscious reasons often seem to be involved in the individual's choice of husband or wife. Oldest or older children tend to select spouses who are younger or youngest children and the opposite may also be true.[2] This does not necessarily mean that the marriage will be a happier one than a marriage with a spouse from another sibling role. The specificity of selection is an attempt by the individual to recapture a childhood situation in which he felt comfortable.

Occupations frequently appear to be chosen so that individuals can carry on successful childhood patterns of sibling relationships. Oldest sisters from large families have been found to select pediatric nursing as a career more frequently than youngest sisters do. Usually, however, choice of occupation is likely to be determined by many factors such as imitation of parents, available family resources, family influences, availability of jobs, and it is doubtful that direct relationships will be found between occupations and sibling roles. But the personality trends that develop out of the birth order of the individual can influence the ways the individual assumes or accepts supervision and the way he relates to his fellow workers.

Individuals from the various sibling roles tend to differ from each other in the ways they relate to their spouses and to their children. Spouses tend to activate for each other the old ways of relating to siblings while children tend to challenge the identification with parents.

We are going to examine in the following chapters each of the family roles in which individuals can be raised. We are going to talk about some of the ways each role may influence the individual to feel about himself, the choices he makes of friends and spouse, his ways of behaving toward them, and the way he relates to his own children. Since other people tend to accept us in the roles we assume for ourselves, we shall be helped in understanding why other people act toward us as they do. We shall examine some of the special advantages of each role and some of the problems that might arise. Ways to overcome the problems will be suggested.

Information given in chapters other than the one that specifically applies to your growing-up role will help you to understand better why other people think, feel and behave as they do, and you will better be able to arrange your relationships so that they are more satisfactory to you and to others. I was, as you know, the oldest child in my family, and I have learned that if I wish to remain friends with another oldest child, I have to curb my tendency to try to take leadership in every situation.

This book should add to your understanding of why you relate to your fellow workers as you do, whether they are your supervisors, your peers, or are supervised by you. You will understand your spouse better when you have learned something about his or her sibling role. Each role has effects that may be comfortable or uncomfortable to live with and you can learn to value or to adjust to the qualities that your spouse has brought from childhood.

Parents will be interested in learning some of the conditions influencing their children's development and ways to help them avoid tendencies which might make problems for them. You may find it especially helpful to learn that each child has certain specific adjustments to make which grow out of his family place and that he can be expected to develop along some predetermined lines in accordance with his birth order. Information will also be given about the effect of family size on the relationship between parents and children and on the relationship between the children themselves.

Our aim is to develop awareness of the tendencies that grow out of the sibling role and then to use that information for conscious direction and control of our behavior. We can then avoid forcing ourselves and others into unrealistic childhood patterns of relationships which do not satisfy our adult needs.

REFERENCES

1. SEARS, R. R.; MACCOBY, E., and LEVIN, H.: *Patterns of Child Rearing.* Evanston; Row, Peterson, 1957.
2. TOMAN, WALTER: Choices of marriage partners by men coming from monosexual sibling configurations. *Brit J Med Psychol, 37:* 43-46, 1964.
3. FISCHER, ANN: The importance of sibling position in the choice of a career in pediatric nursing. *J Health Hum Behav, 3:*283-288, 1962.

Chapter II

WHAT WAS YOUR PLACE IN YOUR CHILDHOOD FAMILY?

D ID you grow up with brothers and sisters? Or did you grow up as an only child?

If you had one or more siblings,* what was your place among them? Were you the older or the younger of two children? Or the oldest of three or more?

Or were you a middle child among three children, or one of the middle children, if there were more than three children in the family in which you grew to adulthood?

Or were you the last and therefore the youngest child of your parents?

These positions in the family give us the terms of only, oldest or older, middle, and youngest child as used in this book. The one which might sometimes be confusing is that of middle child. A middle child, as we use the term here, is not the child in the very middle except in a three-child family. The term middle child is used to designate any child between the oldest and youngest in a family.

Whatever you were when you were growing up, that is what we speak of as your *place* or *position* in the family. Sometimes the term *ordinal position* is used because the child is first, second, or so on in the family. For the same reason, the child is sometimes said to have a certain *position in the family hierarchy,* on the assumption that Father comes first, then Mother, and then each of the children in turn. The most recent trend has been in the direction of talking about the *birth order* of the individual. I shall be using these terms interchangeably because they all refer to the

---

* The word *sibling* will be much used in this book because it stands for all children of the same parents and substitutes for the long phrase "brothers and sisters."

11

same thing: where the person grew up in his family in relation to the other persons composing that family.

What if You Were an Adopted Child?

A child adopted at birth or shortly thereafter fits into the birth order patterns just as would a biological child of the parents. The first child adopted by the parents will feel and react as only or oldest child; later children, whether adopted or biological, will follow in sequence as middle and youngest.

If, however, the adopted child is brought into the family after he has had an opportunity to develop a pattern of behavior on the basis of an earlier sibling role, he will continue to behave in many ways in accordance with the original role. I might give you the example of a family I will name the Pembrokes. The Pembrokes wanted a brother or sister for Alice, their only child, but they did not decide that adoption was the answer until Alice was seven years old. At that time a tragic accident left Geoffrey, the eight year old child of friends, an orphan. His one aunt was not married and felt incapable of assuming responsibility for him. With her consent, the Pembrokes brought him into their home with the approval of the courts and with the intention of formally adopting him after the usual trial period. There was soon much "trouble in paradise." Neither only child wished to share the parents or the home with the other. Alice constantly urged her parents to "send that boy back to his own home." Geoffrey constantly expressed the wish to "get away from that girl." Fortunately his aunt decided that she would like to make a home for him, and he once again became an only child. The Pembrokes settled down with relief with their only child and vowed to be satisfied.

Alice and Geoffrey were too old to change their ways as only children without a period of helpful guidance. I would say that any child who is more than two years of age cannot be brought into a new home without some carry-over of earlier role patterns.

What if You Were a Stepchild?

Things can be very complicated when stepchildren are involved. As with adoptive children, much depends upon the age at which the new mother or father is acquired by the stepchild. The child, of course, will bring into the new home the role he acquired in his previous parental situation, and he will continue to relate to his full brothers and sisters as oldest, middle, or youngest child. If he has been an only child and there are no children in his new family, he will continue to act as an only child until he has to become older or oldest because more children are born. The adjustment of the first child from being only to oldest is always difficult; it is perhaps more difficult for a stepchild than for other children because he usually does not feel wholly attached to the new parent. It will take very careful handling on the part of both parents, biological and step-, to make him feel at home in the new situation. Time, understanding, patience, and affection (with a bit of humor mixed in) will finally do the trick, however.

If the child is relatively young, the adjustment may be rapid because he has one parent present with whom he developed his role and who will give him confidence in adjusting to the new situation. For example, a widower with a five year old son married a divorcee who also had only one child, a three year old son. It was not long before the two boys had fitted nicely into the pattern of older brother and younger brother.

There is a special condition to be considered when evaluating the relationship which stepchildren have with their stepbrothers and sisters. It seems to make a difference whether the original parent remaining to the child is his father or his mother. If the child obtains a new mother, i.e., a stepmother, he sometimes finds it more difficult to fit into the new family pattern than if he brings his original mother with him and has a stepfather. Mothers tend to relate to their biological first children in a special way, even though there may be older stepchildren present. The case of Sigmund Freud is an example. When he was born, there were already in the home a much older stepbrother and two children of that stepbrother. But he was the first child of his mother and she reacted fully to him as though he was the first child in the family. Sigmund was very much the oldest child of her final total of seven biological children.[1]

REFERENCE

1. BAKER, RACHEL: *Sigmund Freud for Everybody*. New York, Popular Library, 1952.

Chapter III

IS BEING BORN AN ADULT
THE ONLY WAY OUT?

A FRIEND sent me a statement to the effect that "Modern psychology tells us that it is bad to be an orphan, terrible to be an only child, damaging to be the youngest, crushing to be in the middle, and taxing to be the oldest. There seems to be no way, except to be born an adult!"[1]

The sibling role cannot be held responsible for all the challenges that the individual must meet in growing from neonate to adult. The personality and behavior that make you into the unique adult individual you are grow out of many causes.

Heredity

From a line of ancestors comes the physiology of the individual which begins to form at the moment he is conceived. The temperament of the individual, the speed with which he reacts, the extent of sensitivity to outside stimuli, may largely depend upon heredity. Certainly clear-cut differences are seen among babes just born in the amount of general body movement and in the extent to which they react to noises and outside distractions. In a study by Estella Chess and others[2] and reported in the book *Your Child is a Person,* these differences were found to persist throughout the ten-year period of their observation of the same children. The chances are that they persist throughout an individual's lifetime.

Most parents are going to react differently to their children in terms of these differences in activity, irritability, and sensitivity. My older son, for instance, tends toward quick reactions and a great deal of activity. I tend to be slow and more or less deliberate in my behavior, and so does my second son. Through the years, I have frequently heard my first son protest, "Mother, you are so slow!" And I have frequently said to him, "Take it easy now!" We

14

have all tried to accept each other as we are in this respect and make the best of it, and I recommend this for any parent.

Earliest Environmental Influences

Even before the infant is born, the outside world begins to influence his development. The conditions surrounding the mother influence her diet and physiological state during pregnancy, which, in turn, may have some effect on the developing fetus. The mother's emotional state, a reaction to conditions surrounding her in some cases, may also influence the development of the child she is carrying.

It is possible that birth order may have some effect on the individual's development even as he is still unborn. Some authorities believe that each pregnancy of the mother may change the intrauterine conditions for each following child. The specific results of such changes have yet to be established, however.

Birth conditions may themselves be affected by the birth order of the child coming into the world. The duration of labor has been reported as much as fifty percent higher for first-born children, and the point has been made that they may therefore be subject to a higher degree of cerebral compression. Forceps are often necessary at the birth of first children and such deliveries tend to be more hazardous than easier later births. In at least one study, children with instrumental births displayed physical elements of restlessness, distractibility, and irritable hyperactivity to a greater extent than children spontaneously delivered.[3]

It is therefore possible that some of the differences we find between first-born children and later-born children may be the result of varying physical conditions of the mother and problems besetting first pregnancies and labor.

Parents

Human beings are usually raised in family situations with two adults who are responsible for our well-being and our development until we have gained strength, capacity, and training to take responsibility for ourselves. If the biological parents of the child are not able (or willing) to assume the parental responsibilities, the child is placed in situations where there are substitutes to care for him. These parents may be adoptive or stepparents who are essentially the same in their influence as the biological parents, if the child is placed in their care at an early age.

The parents are of primary importance in determining the kind of family atmosphere in which they and their children live. Just as each individual comes to have his own emotional approach to living and certain values and standards that guide his behavior, so each family has its own individual emotional tone, its own set of values and standards, and each member of the family reacts to them.

The parents establish a pattern of behavior and attitudes for themselves and for their children. This pattern reflects the parents' financial resources and the social and cultural levels they have inherited or acquired. Their intellectual interests and their educational levels have much to do with determining the intellectual aspirations, interests, and attainments of all the children in their family.

They set the emotional tone of the family through their own emotional reactions and their relationship with each other. If they are emotionally and intellectually controlled people, the family atmosphere is likely to be one of quiet, cool objectivity, and all the children in the family are likely to be relatively more controlled and objective than many of their neighborhood and school friends. If the parents are warm and friendly both with each other and with their children, then all their children are likely to be. If the family atmosphere is charged with emotional display by the parents, all the children in that family are likely to express their emotions rather freely.

The relationship between the parents has perhaps more to do with what we may call the *family style of life* than any other aspect of the parents' behavior. If there is tolerance, respect, affection between the parents, all of the children are likely to reflect these characteristics both in their own personalities and in their relationships with each other. Peace is likely to be a word that can be applied to the "style" of such a family. If, on the other hand, there is constant display of anger on the part of one or both parents, if their relationship with each other reflects basic disagreements between them, the family style will be disturbed and tense no matter how kindly and pleasant one or both of the parents may be in other situations.

Parents transmit to us the basic characteristics of our personalities. We learn to be orderly or messy, optimistic or gloomy, irritable or calm, from identification with them and from the general atmosphere they establish in the homes. If they have helped us to be kind, gentle, affectionate, that is generally how we will be in any place in the family. The sibling role will often determine the relative extent of our kindness and gentleness compared with other members of the family. For instance, oldest children in all families tend to be relatively more angry and tense than their siblings, but the eldest child in a happy, peaceful family may seem as calm as a Buddha compared with the eldest child from an emotional family.

The composition of the family, the atmosphere of the family, efforts made by the parents, can all change the impact of the sibling role on the development of the child.

Other Family Conditions Which May Influence Birth Order Effects

Isolation of a family, as on a farm, may intensify the pattern of differences between children in the various birth order positions. In one large family, which was for many years isolated on a Midwestern farm, the oldest of the eight children was clearly a "third parent" to his younger brothers and sisters. Still, after fifty years, they frequently turn to him for advice. The youngest child is still called "Babe" by her siblings.

Social isolation does not occur only on farms. It can exist in wealthy urban areas where there is little neighborhood interaction between children. In some suburban areas the intensity of experience of the sibling role seems diluted by the intermingling of the children during their early years with many other neighborhood children.

The cultural origins of the parents may affect their expectations of the role to be taken by each child in their family. Some families are influenced by backgrounds in which the oldest male is expected to take over the occupation of the father and to assume his responsibilities when the father must give them up. Often in such families an oldest girl is made responsible for taking on the role of mother substitute and helper.

It will be noted that the above influences either dilute or increase the effect of being in a certain place in the family. They do not negate or reverse the effects.

Circumstances involving parents may change the role of a child in a specific position in the family. Death of a parent of either sex may force the oldest child of the same sex to take on a parental role regardless of where that child is in the family hierarchy. For instance, after the death of her mother, an only girl in a family became a kind of "little mother" to her brothers although two were older than she. A divorce may also change the effect of the sibling place, particularly for the child of opposite sex from the parent remaining in custody of the children.

Attitudes of a parent that grow out of his childhood role may cause the parent to raise his children in such a way that the effect of the place in the family is somewhat changed for each of them. A woman grew up as the oldest of three children, the two younger siblings being boys. Since her mother was ill, she assumed much responsibility for mothering her brothers. After she married and had two sons of her own, she maintained such strict control over them that the older did not assume the full characteristics of an older child. He became in effect a middle child in a family that reestablished the childhood role of the mother.

Conditions Involving the Children in the Family

SEX OF THE CHILDREN. The first child of his sex in any family may assume many of the responsibilities and characteristics of an oldest child.

The intensity of the effect of place in the family increases when all the children are of the same sex. The younger sister of a girl, for instance, is likely to feel more intensely the effects of being younger than is the younger sister of a boy. In the latter case, the younger child is likely to be asked to take over some of the "mothering" responsibilities of the family, and she is likely to emphasize her sexual difference from her brother rather than the age difference.

Evidence is increasing that the sex of the child immediately preceding or following another child can be of great importance in determining characteristics and behavior of both children. A recent study by Dr. William T. Smelser and Dr. Louis H. Stewart[4] suggests that the educational level attained by a first child in a family may be strongly related to the sex of the child following him in the family. In this study, the older of two children completed a significantly greater number of years of education than the sibling, only if that sibling were of opposite sex. It will be noted that the emphasis in the chapters on two-child families is on the attitudes and relationships of the children, and the adjustments described are such that they would be expected to bring about the differences in educational achievement reported by Dr. Smelser and Dr. Stewart.

DEATH, DISABILITY, OR OTHER SPECIAL CONDITIONS OF A CHILD IN THE FAMILY. Death of a brother or sister will shift the position of the next younger or older child, with the effect being relatively less if the next older or younger is more than three years old when the death occurs. In other words, if the oldest child in a family dies, the next child in line may take over many of the responsibilities and therefore the attitudes of first child.

Other special conditions involving a child in a family may change the birth order effect both for him and for his siblings. It is my opinion that unusual characteristics or conditions of a child make a difference only if they make it difficult or impossible for him to assume the usual responsibilities of the role. For instance, if the first child in a family is mentally retarded or has some physical disability that severely limits his activities, he may not develop as does the usual oldest child. If he remains an only child or is a youngest child, he is likely in most aspects to display the characteristics of his role in the family. Mental retardation is likely to be more effective in changing aspects of a sibling role than is physical disability. Siblings of a child with mental retardation are likely to act as though he does not exist as a competitor; certainly he cannot assume the responsibilities that an oldest child usually assumes. Thus the second child in the family becomes essentially the oldest, and so on down the line of siblings.

If the unusual characteristic of the child is one that enhances his value in the family, such as being unusually gifted intellectually, talented in some special way, or unusually attractive, the child still will assume the aspects of the sibling place he holds. He may be given much more attention by his parents than he usually would receive, but the pattern of relationships with siblings will be the same as for any other child. Arthur M. was the youngest of three children. He was very gifted intellectually. His two older sisters in no way allowed his superior intelligence to affect their "mothering" of him even though they were both of average intelligence. They enhanced the childlike aspects of his position as youngest child by constantly "babying" him because they were so proud of his achievements. On the other hand, Norbert Wiener,[5] the brilliant developer of cybernetics, was the first child in his family. He was recognized to be an intellectual genius by his parents and educators during his early childhood. Nevertheless, when a third child was born into the family while Norbert was in his late teens, he was called upon to assume much responsibility for the care of the baby just as might any other oldest child. (And like many oldest children put in such a position, he thoroughly resented it.)

Dolly L. was the oldest of six children. She was born with a head of bright red hair and features that made her, at two hours of age, the winner of the "beauty contest" in the hospital nursery. Her physical attractiveness continued to make her the "queen" of various social situations from kindergarten pageants to college proms. But at home she was known as "our oldest girl" and she supervised the younger children, helped them with their homework, and helped her mother with the housework just as would any oldest daughter in a family of modest circumstances.

AGE DIFFERENCES BETWEEN THE CHILDREN. An important difference can occur in birth order effects if there is an unusual age spread between siblings. If the first child is an only child for more than six of seven years, he may continue for the rest of his life to be more like an only child than like an older or oldest child. If there is only one younger sibling, that child may develop more as does an only child than as the usual younger brother or sister. In such cases parents frequently recognize the situation by commenting that "We are raising two only children." The child, so isolated by many years from the other children in the family, will often remark that he doesn't feel as though he has any brothers or sisters.

If there is a large age gap between one group of children in a family and a later group, as sometimes occurs when death or divorce separates spouses and the surviving spouse remarries, the first child of the second family will be more like an oldest child than a later child. Sigmund Freud and George Washington both grew up under such conditions.

Rarely, however, does the mantle of oldest child fall with full strength upon any later child. The acceptance of responsibility can be great, but it is usually experienced with more relaxation by the later child than by the actual first child in the family. Any later child does not receive in full strength the pressures and requirements of the parents. These are mitigated by the very existence of an older child, even though he is unable to carry the full responsibilities of his situation.

The Role of the Society in Which the Family Lives

At this point we must consider the extent to which the effects of being in a certain place in the family hierarchy might be influenced by the cultural environment in which it exists. We are aware of the many groups living in the United States and, to a lesser extent, in other countries with social structures modeled largely on the European pattern. In the United States we have groups which can be labeled upper class, upper middle class, lower middle class, lower class. We have the ultra-wealthy, the wealthy, the comfortably self-sufficient wage earners, the more or less comfortable recipients of aid of one kind or another, and the poverty stricken. All races are represented and original national origins of families are as varied as the nations of the earth.

To what extent, then, can we apply our findings about birth order effects to any one individual in the United States whose way of life might be influenced by any of these cultural and economic conditions. Or, for that matter, can the findings be applied to an individual living in another country?

To answer these questions we must first consider the source of birth order effects. The writer has claimed that they grow out of the interplay of family members in the usual family setting. The usual family is made up of parents and children living in quarters more or less separated from those of other families. As the family members live together, they take on certain roles that depend to a great extent on inherent conditions that cannot be changed: age differences and the effects of age differences. At any one time, the members of the family differ from each other physically, in intellectual level, and in general capabilities. This basic pattern exists to some degree wherever the human species lives and thrives. It seems probable that our cave-mother ancestor, busy suckling the latest baby, conveyed in some way to her four-year-old son that he had better put another branch on the fire, and then he could go check on the whereabouts of his two-year-old brother. Out of such a pattern of relationships the roles of first-born and later-born probably could be defined even at a primitive point in human history.

Some societies may live more communally than others, and there are differences in the extent to which the biological father is considered to be an important part of the intimate family unit. But to the extent that there is isolation of one family unit from another, we can expect to find adults and children falling into role patterns dependent upon age differences which will be reflected in their attitudes toward themselves and toward each other.

We may, then, make a first generalization about birth order effects. It is that the members of a family will show differences which will depend upon their places in the family hierarchy in any culture which isolates family groups from each other. Thus there will be birth order effects in any culture in which there is stability of the family pattern.

We now come to another generalization: birth order effects will be similar in all cultures, insofar as there are similarities between those cultures in family patterns and interactions. This requires, of course, that we apply findings concerning birth order effects to another culture, only if that culture does have the same basic family pattern.

In our society we tend to emphasize the role of eldest child and particularly that of the first son, but we do not do so to the extent that other societies do. In India, for instance, the oldest son is given unusual family responsibilities and is subject to severe parental pressures of expectations and aspirations. This may be one reason that schizophrenia has been reported[6] to occur more frequently among early-born than later-born children in that country, while in England and the United States no consistent relationship has been found with birth order. Among Japanese families which derive their income from family-owned businesses, schizophrenia has been found to occur more frequently among the oldest sons and the youngest daughters. It was suggested that the reason might be that in such Japanese families the roles of oldest son and youngest daughter carry unusual responsibilities.[7]

Israeli boys raised in Kibbutz situations were compared, by A. I. Rabin,[8] with children living with their families in agricultural villages where the structure of the family is much like ours. The Kibbutz boys are placed shortly after birth in "children's houses" where they live with other children in the care of nurses, thus leaving both mothers and fathers free to contribute their help in the development of the country. It was found that the Kibbutz-reared children were more likely than the others to think of siblings in positive and constructive relationships with each other, and they did not place as much emphasis on hostility between siblings.

From such studies we learn that the role taken by the family members and their attitudes toward each other will depend upon the requirements of the society for family organization. This, of course, suggests that we should not expect to be able to apply the generalizations in this book to individuals raised in cultures where the family structure is different from the usual one in the United States without taking these differences into account.

Now we come to the effects of birth order in our own country. It has been suggested that our findings may hold only for middle class, urban, white Americans, or for persons with the same characteristics in other countries, also strongly influenced in their social and political organization by European values and cultural patterns.

We have stated that birth order effects depend upon stability of family patterns and that they will be similar insofar as the family patterns and interactions are similar. In general, the same family pattern exists at all levels of society in this country. It is for this reason that we find similar trends among research results, although the subjects used have represented many different economic and social groups. The subjects used in research projects have come from both lower and middle-class families represented in the public schools, state colleges and universities and from upper middle-class and upper class families represented in large numbers in private elementary and high schools and such universities as Harvard and Yale. The results of these studies suggest that the cultural values of our society take priority over the forces at play on groups within the society, insofar as the larger effects of birth order are concerned. Autobiographies of the wealthy, the great, the status people, reflect the same trends as the self-revelations of those originally less gifted by the gods. Clinical observation of individuals raised in varied socioeconomic levels show birth order effects along the same lines as those presented here.

However, when we are studying birth order effects in any one society, we need not necessarily be interested only in those effects which are dependent on basic and largely unchanging conditions. If our interest in birth order is related to our wish to understand ourselves, we will also want to know how such variable conditions, such as socio-economic differences might influence the development of children in various positions in the family.

One of the most frequent areas of study has been the effect of birth order on the educational level achieved by children growing up in various family positions. Obviously one reason for such concentration of interest is the ready availability of the subjects and information about them for the research people in institutions of learning. It has been of some interest to find that the first children can be expected to achieve at a higher educational level than the later children in families. These findings have allowed us to understand and to predict a bit better the achievement to be expected for first children in general.

Obviously, however, socio-economic conditions of the family would have a strong influence on the level of education to be acquired by children in a family. If we try to apply the generalization that first-born children tend to achieve at a higher educational level to *all* first-born children, we find ourselves in trouble. A first-born child from a large family has often been found to obtain less education than a last-born child from such a family. Since large families tend to be associated with lower socioeconomic level, it is probable that the economic circumstances of the large family change the birth order effects. It is always important, then, to clarify whether a specific effect is strongly influenced by factors other than the role in the family determined by the birth order.

Fortunately research in the field of birth order is becoming more refined and defined. The study mentioned previously by Dr. Smelser and Dr. Stewart shows how research results can be better defined if research variables are carefully controlled. By holding socioeconomic conditions constant, these researchers were able to reveal the fact that the older child of two obtains a higher level of education, only if he or she is followed by a sibling of opposite sex. Thus a very important step was taken in improving understanding of birth order effects.*

Educational level, like any other condition dependent upon variables in society, can be expected to change as an effect of birth order whenever the socioeconomic conditions affecting family life change. As these conditions improve for all families and all children in our society, it is probable that little difference will be found on this variable for first and later children.

Another generalization, then, is that birth order effects reflect any characteristics of a culture which influences the interaction of family members with each other; birth order effects will change as those conditions change.

Limits Placed on Interpretation of Birth Order Effects

The writer has given little more than passing attention to studies attempting to relate birth order to such complicated conditions as psychosis, delinquency, neuroticism, and depression. These conditions grow out of many complicated causes which are not yet fully defined. Psychotic reactions, for instance, may have multiple causes, some of which may not be related to the interaction among family members. The symptoms of depression and addiction are also not yet understood as far as causality is concerned. They appear to be ways utilized by an individual to defend himself from anger and tension stemming from many causes which differ from individual to individual. Let us take as an example a very depressed young woman. She may be depressed because she feels unable to

---

* It will be noted that the statements made by the writer concerning two-child families permit prediction of the results found in this study.

achieve at a level expected by her parents, in which case she is likely to be a first-born child. Or she may be depressed because her husband neglects her, in which case she is likely to be an only or last-born child.

Many persons addicted to alcohol make tremendous demands on themselves for achievement at a perfect level and thus are likely to have been first-born in their families. On the other hand, we have research results that suggest that a last-born child who has lost a parent in early childhood may turn to alcohol as a means of alleviating tension and depression.

It is very important to differentiate between reactions which grow specifically out of the social interrelationships in the family unit and symptomological reactions which may be due to many causes.

The writer has described, in some instances, personality trends related to birth order without being able to refer to research findings which fully substantiate these conclusions. Such generalizations have been drawn from clinical observations of many persons and have been made only when they seemed well supported by such evidence. Research studies attempting to compare persons from birth order positions in relation to personality characteristics have suffered from two great limitations. One is the lack of ways to evaluate such characteristics with either validity or reliability. Another is the use of subjects in such studies who represent various birth order positions but do not come from the same families. Since the parents tend to establish the modes of emotional expression for the children in a family, all the children tend to express themselves at much the same level with the effects of birth position showing only relative differences. For instance, a youngest child from a family which fosters "dominance" might be comparatively more dominant in behavior than an eldest child from a family in which self-effacement was encouraged. But this dominant youngest child might be comparatively less dominant than the older children in his family. If the study does not compare children within the same family with each other, the results can only show how representatives of different families compare with each other on the characteristics studied.

In this chapter I have described some of the various conditions which may change the way the child experiences nis particular place in the family hierarchy. You will want to evaluate your own sibling role in terms of the conditions which surrounded you as you grew up.

The fact that such conditions make a difference causes us to recognize that there is nothing fixed nor inevitable about the effect of being born into a certain place in a family. The pattern tends to be the same for children and adults born into certain family places because parents and families tend to follow certain patterns of behavior. If parents become aware that they tend to take certain attitudes toward the children holding specific positions in the family, they can change their attitudes and methods so that their children will experience no serious problems growing out of birth order. Adults raised in specific family places can, if they come to understand how birth order has directed their development, change their behavior to conform with current reality rather than with fantasied sibling and parental demands.

REFERENCES

1. My thanks to Jean Mary Orme-Johnson.
2. CHESS, ESTELLA; THOMAS, ALEXANDER, and BIRCH, HERBERT B.: *Your Child is a Person.* New York, Viking Pr, 1965.
3. WILE, 1. S., and DAVIS, ROSE: The relation of birth to behavior. In Kluckholm, Clyde, and Murray, Henry A., Editors: *Personality in Nature, Society, and Culture.* New York, Knopf, 1948.
4. SMELSER, WILLIAM T., and STEWART, LOUIS H.: Where are the siblings? *Sociometry, 31:*294-303, 1968.
5. WIENER, NORBERT: *Ex-Prodigy.* New York, Simon & Schuster, 1953.
6. BARRY, HERBERT, III, and BARRY, HERBERT, JR.: Birth order, family size, and schizophrenia. *Arch Gen Psychiat, 17:*435-440, 1967.
7. CAUDILL, W.: Sibling rank and style of life among Japanese psychiatric patients. *Folia Psychiat Neurolo Jap, Suppl. 7,* 1964.
8. RABIN, A. I.: Some psychosexual differences between Kibbutz and non-Kibbutz Israeli boys. *J Project Techn, 22:*328-332, 1958.

Chapter IV

GENERAL DIFFERENCES BETWEEN FIRST CHILDREN AND LATER CHILDREN

A LL families, of course, must have a first child if they are to have any at all. That child may or may not be followed by one or more children. If he is not, he remains an only child. If he is followed by other children, he becomes the older of two children, or the oldest of three or more.

We are going to find that there are very important differences between those first children who are followed by siblings and those who are not. We are also going to learn that there are important differences between later children according to their specific positions in the family. However, the results of the many experimental studies, comparing all first children with later children in families, have shown us that there are big general differences to be expected between all first children and all later children; we can better understand ourselves and our children if we are aware of these differences.

The studies, too, have given us some indication of the reasons the differences come about. As we shall discover, they develop largely out of the interaction between child and parent. As we understand better how this interaction can make differences between first children and later children, we shall better understand how the differences come about between children from each of the ordinal positions in the family.

The Parents of the First Child in the Family

Let us look at that couple who are welcoming their first child into their home. That couple might be you and your husband or wife—or it might be your mother and father back in the "olden" days before you were born.

There are usually stars in the eyes of both prospective or new parents, stars that get their sparkle from the delight, pride, and excitement they feel at the advent of this miracle: the arrival of their first child. But there are likely to be other feelings, too. They may feel very tense and anxious about their ability to take care of the baby. The mother, particularly, may be frightened and apprehensive. Perhaps she has had to push away some regrets that she has to take on new responsibilities and lose some of her freedom. Perhaps she wonders if she is able to do what is necessary just to keep alive this seemingly most fragile bit of humanity. In any case, both parents are going to take very seriously anything the infant does and usually will make very strenuous attempts to learn the best ways to cope with him.

They have probably come to the point of being parents with many preconceptions about what it is to be a parent. Most new parents are sure that they know ways of greatly improving on the job their parents did in raising them. Such neat ideas often cause us to smile in later years of being parents. By that time we are aware that all of us usually "learn what it is to be parents only after we are parents ourselves."

The new parents may not have a wholly realistic view of the difficulties involved in the business of raising a child from infancy to maturity. A woman recently commented to me that she remembered as a child being surprised when her grandmother commented, "If I've done nothing else in this world, I've raised four good children." The woman said that she thought then that her grandmother was making much out of what was no achievement at all. Obviously children just grow up! The memory brought a wry smile because it came to her in the course of a discussion about her present problems in raising her own youngsters.

Whether their ideas are realistic or not, new parents usually have firm notions about the way their child should behave and develop. They may have high expectations for his achievement, from the way he is to react to toilet training to the honors he is to receive when he graduates from college.

These, then, are some of the pressures to which the first child is subjected just because he is the first. It is important to keep in mind, too, that he is always the only child in the family for a period of time. That means that he and he alone is the recipient of all the loving and well-meaning attention of his parents—and the sole recipient of their pressures and admonitions too.

If the first child is to be understood, we must also keep in mind that he never loses his position of first child no matter how many later children are born. All through his growing years at home he continues to present his parents with "first-time" problems. As my mother said years ago in sympathetic response to my first-child complaints, "The first child is a guinea pig for the parents' experimentation in raising children."

The Parents of the Later Children in the Same Family

When the next child comes along, the parents have been changed by the experience of having the first child. They may not welcome the later children with the same delight they exhibited with their first, but they also do not meet him with the same apprehension and anxiety. They are more confident; they have learned that they can keep a child alive and well and that sometimes he seems to grow almost despite them.

They usually have also become more realistic in their demands for "normal" development and achievement on the part of the child. They understand children better; they better know their limitations and what is to be expected in the way of childish behavior.

Nor do they usually direct as much attention and time toward the second or later children as they did toward the first. They cannot, because there is the first child with his continuing requirements to share their time and attention. The parents rarely have a relationship with a later child that is as intense and close as their relationship with their first child. This is true even when a parent may feel a real preference for a later child and establish an unusually close relationship with him. The condition of being the "only child" is never there for the later child in the usual family situation.

The Differences in the First and Later Children as a Result of the Changes in Parents

In an earlier chapter we talked about the differences among children that seem to be due to heredity and perhaps to physiological and biological conditions of the mother. We said then that the general "temperament" of the individual seems largely to be a predetermined and fixed characteristic which remains the same throughout his lifetime. We also said that the general atmosphere of the family life has a great deal to do with whether or not the person is, on the whole, a kind, pleasant, winning person. In other words, many of the qualities that we call "personality" seem to develop *outside* of the sibling situation.

Nevertheless, the parents, while remaining the same people and hence having the same general influence on the development of all their children, tend to treat their children differently according to whether or not those children are first or later children. Accordingly, we should expect to find that the children in the same family would show relative differences among themselves in certain personality characteristics. For instance, if the Johnsons are volatile, angry people, all of their children might more quickly become angry and emotional than the kids in the Jones' family because the Jones' are patient and controlled in their general personalities. However, if sibling place makes a difference, we might expect the first Johnson child and the first Jones' child to differ in the same direction in relation to their siblings in the personality characteristics of angry responsiveness and emotional upheaval.

And so it seems to be. Here are some of the differences that have been suggested between first-born and later-born children in the same families.

Anger

One of the first observations I made of first-born children and adults was that they seemed relatively more angry and irritable than their younger siblings. Often their approach to the outside world seemed more hostile and critical than that of the other children in their families.

Various conditions of development for the first-born would suggest reasons that he might be more easily angered than his siblings. Parents seem to display more anger in their relations with their first-born children than they do toward later-borns.[1] Physical punishment seems more often to be used by parents in disciplining their first-born children than in disciplining their later children.[2]

On the other hand, first-born children and adults do not tend to be as outwardly aggressive in behavior as later-borns do, according to recent studies reviewed by Dr. Edward E. Sampson.[3] Even if this is true, we cannot conclude that later-borns feel as angry inside as first-borns might. We should not confuse an inner state of tension and anger with outer physical aggressiveness. We would expect later-borns to exhibit more overt physical aggressiveness because they apparently tend to use muscular and other physical means of coping with the environment more readily than does the first-born.[4] First-borns tend to express their feelings verbally rather than physically.

Fearfulness and Cautiousness

First-born children seem often to be more fearful and anxious than later-born children.

How does this develop out of the way they are treated by their parents? Parents have been found to treat their first children with more anxiety, more interference, and more restrictiveness than they do their later children. On the other hand, they tend at the same time to treat their first children with less protectiveness than their later children. They tend to be much more solicitous of the welfare of their later children than of the first.[1]

What seems to happen is that they are anxious about the well being of their first child and they have time to supervise him, but they are not aware of some of the real dangers that can confront an infant and small child. They also (remember?) have high hopes and firm ideas about making a small paragon of this child. I remember, for example, shivering as I saw a young couple carrying a shoeless infant through the December cold. The mother assured me earnestly that they thought it was a good idea to help their baby become "tough" and able physically to withstand the affronts of nature. A severe case of flu almost took their baby from them during the spring. I have noticed that all their later children have always been well shod.

First-born children, then, become more fearful in response to their parents' fearfulness and anxiety. At the same time they learn to be more cautious in general. Dr. Stanley Schachter,[5] one of the chief investigators in the field of birth order effects, found that first-born college students reacted with more fearfulness in experimental situations than later-born students did. He considered that fearfulness also caused them to drop out of the anxiety-provoking situations, i.e., they refused to continue as subjects more often than did later-born students. It seems to me that this behavior might also be interpreted as cautiousness. Dr. Schachter also tells us of evidence that first-born children are less likely to be effective fighter pilots of planes than later-born children. Again I consider this cautiousness which develops in response to anxiety and fearfulness.

Being Stubborn and Strong-Willed

Parents seem to treat their first-born children with more restrictiveness and more interference than they do their later children. This may be a reason that the first-born child seems to be more strong-willed and stubborn than later children. Parents tend to be relatively intolerant of his childish behavior. He has to learn to defend his wishes if he is to develop along individual lines. Another reason may be that inexperienced parents are often uncertain of their judgments and hence will be inconsistent with their first child. He learns that if he insists upon his way and is persistent, he is likely to wear them down.

I believe that it is this trend in parental control of the first-born child that sometimes develops his persistence and stubbornness into outright rebelliousness at a later date. Many studies have given us reason to believe that the first-born child is more likely than later-borns to engage in such "offenses against the home" as running away, dropping out of school and refusing to obey parents. These activities may often grow out of an early situation in which the child pitted his will against that of an uncertain and ambivalent parent.

Conscience or Super-Ego

Parents bring to their children standards of "right" behavior and "effective" behavior. They train their children, or try to do so, in moral conduct such as adherence to honesty, fair dealings with others and truthfulness. They teach or serve as examples for taking responsibility for oneself and others, for making oneself useful to society, and earning one's livelihood. They believe that certain levels of achievement are important and they have ideas about how these levels are to be reached.

Parents place pressure on their children to behave properly during early years. Later they press for the best possible school achievement and efficient training for occupational success. The child wants to please his parents and to enhance his own status. At first he imitates his parents and follows their admonitions and instructions. Gradually their standards become part of his own thinking. He begins to approve or disapprove of his behavior insofar as it accords or does not accord with those standards and we say that he has developed a "conscience." Henceforth he will be guided by his own conscience rather than by the admonitions of his parents.

We have said that parents tend to be more extreme and intolerant in their expectations for the conduct and achievement of their first child than they may be with later-born children. The impact of their personalities and standards seems to be maximum for that first child because he alone is the object of their attention for a period of time. Consequently only children and oldest children often seem to be more conforming to the standards of their parents than do later-born children. It also seems that they tend to be more self-critical and that their consciences are more severe in establishing self-disapproval. First-born boys among a group studied at Harvard University were considered to display more demanding consciences than later-born boys did. They also saw their fathers as strict, authoritarian, demanding, aggressive and punishing. Apparently the inhibitory and disciplinarian attitudes of their fathers had been incorporated as standards with which they guided their own conduct.[2]

If you should care to listen carefully to the speech of other people, you can often pick out people who are first-born by noting the words they use and the attitudes they express. First-borns frequently use words like "should" and "ought to." They may suggest that "it would be wise to do thus and so." Such admonitions are reflections of their consciences, of their frequent belief that there is one right way to do things and it should be followed.

If all goes well, the first-born child can be expected to move gradually in the direction of conformity with his parent's requirements, despite much verbal rebelliousness along the way. Thus first-born children tend to be generally more socially conforming in their early adulthood. First-born college students appear to conform more readily to opinions held by a group as a whole and to be more responsive to the suggestions of others than are later-born children. Through introjection of the parents' standards, they have developed a tendency to be socially conforming rather than rebellious.[6]

The strength of conscience in determining the adult behavior of the individual might be suggested by a recent study of "honesty" of subjects in relation to their birth order. Male students were asked not to talk to others about research in which they were participating and their promises were obtained that they would not do so. In a follow-up of those who remained "honest" and those who did not, first-born subjects were found to have talked to fewer persons than did later-born students.[7]

The personality disorder termed *obsessive-compulsive* is usually considered to be related to excessive superego (conscience) development. In a recent study, an overwhelmingly large proportion of a group of patients under observation were found to be first-born.[8]

Verbal and Scholastic Achievement

The close relationship between parents and their first child offers opportunities which might be considered advantageous for the child in some ways. First-borns tend to develop better verbal skills on the whole than do later-born children.[9] This may be the result of more verbal communication between parents and their one child than between parents and each of their later children. It is undoubtedly in accordance with their better verbal skills that first-born children are usually found to make higher grades through high school and college than do later-born children.[10]

No corresponding superiority has been found for the mathematical aptitude of first-born children.[11] Since parents do not usually interact with their children by the use of mathematical concepts and symbols, the finding is in accordance with the theory that it is the verbal communication between first child and parents that develops the greater verbal skill of the first-born.

A number of studies of college students have suggested that the first-born child is more likely than later-born to attend college. Between 1960 and 1963 over sixty percent of students entering the University of California at Santa Barbara were first-born, according to William D. Altus.[12] If the proportion were in accordance with the proportions of first-born in the general population, we would expect about one-third of the students to be first-born.[13] More first-born than later-born sons have been found among students in a medical school.[14]

It seems to be fairly well established that eminent men, particularly those who are eminent because of their scholarship and scientific achievement, are more likely to be first-born than later-born children.[15]

Attitudes Toward Achievement

First-born college students have been found to maintain higher needs for achievement than later-born students sometimes do.[16] There is even evidence that first-born females in the United States might sometimes have an even higher need for achievement than their male counterparts.[16] Clinical observation suggests that the female first-born child will often be heiress to the ambitions of a mother who disdains the housekeeping interests of the "feminine mystique," and who imposes on her daughter her own desires for intellectual and vocational achievement outside the home.

First-born students have been found to meet the prerequisites of their classes with what might be greater conscientiousness than has been shown by the later-born students in these studies. On the hypothesis that volunteering to be subjects in college experiments indicates a serious interest in participation in the learning experience, investigators have compared the proportions of first-born and later-born students who do volunteer. The results are not clear-cut, but usually first-borns have been found to display what seemed to be more readiness to participate as volunteers.[17] Perhaps the most likely situation is that first-born students are more inclined to volunteer when being a subject is highly recommended but not necessarily required, as has been found in a recent study.[18] They then do what *should* be done, according to their consciences.

An Interesting Study of the Differences in Consciences and Approach of First-Born and Later-Born Students

[Later-born children have been found to be more interested in relationships with other people than in achievement, in contrast with their older siblings.[19] We have just reviewed findings that suggest that the first-born is not only interested in achievement, but that he tends to achieve at a higher level educationally and perhaps in occupational areas where scholastic attainment is important.]

A study was made by Dr. Jerome E. Singer into the complicated interplay of social relationships, academic achievement, and attitudes of first-born and later-born children.[20] Dr. Singer's approach was to study the relationship between the grades attained by male students and the ability of these same students to be "socially manipulative" as measured by a standard test. No relationship was found between the grades of the first-born students and the levels they reached in "social manipulation." It might therefore be assumed that the higher grades of first-born students were obtained, not through "social manipulation," but as the result of the classic application of intellectual abilities and effort. But there was found to be a strong relationship between the grades of later-born males and their scores in "social manipulation." It might then be assumed that later-born males who obtain higher grades may do so by impressing their teachers in ways that do not involve the classic application of intellectual abilities and effort alone.

Now we know about boys. What about the girls?

In a previous study Dr. Singer had concentrated on another aspect of the development of the college student: his or her physical attributes. He had found evidence that first-born girls had a more accurate perception of their own physical attributes than did later-born girls. They knew, for instance, better than did the later-born girls where they stood in relation to usual standards of physical attractiveness.[21]

Dr. Singer studied the girls' grades in relation to their abilities to be "socially manipulative." He found no relation between grade levels and level of "social manipulativeness" for either first-born or later-born girls. But the fact was evident that first-born girls made higher grades. Dr. Singer did not assume that intellectual effort alone was the cause. Further study showed that there was a significant relationship between the physical attractiveness of a first-born girl and the grades she made. Somehow a first-born girl who was attractive tended to obtain higher grades than those who were not physically attractive. Since Dr. Singer already knew that first-born girls had a relatively more accurate perception of their physical attributes than did later-born girls, he wondered if somehow the first-born girls might use this knowledge in such a way as to affect their grade levels. It seemed possible that the more physically attractive first-born girls might quite knowingly use their attractiveness to influence professors to give them "the benefit of the doubt" when grades came along.

Dr. Singer's next question was most logical in view of the large classes in today's universities. How could first-born girls ensure that instructors not only noticed them but came to know their names so that grades could be properly recorded? He learned that first-born girls did, indeed, find a way! He discovered that they tended to sit in the front rows of classes, that they more frequently talked with the instructors in the classroom after classes, and that they took occasion to confer with them in their offices more often than later-born girls!

My interpretation of this behavior of first-born girls is somewhat different than that made by Dr. Singer. First-born girls have also been found to be relatively achievement oriented and to have a good level of verbal intelligence. Perhaps the first-born girls, both those who are attractive and those who are not, are originally more aggressive in their attempts to get good grades by contacting the instructors. Perhaps this aggressiveness doesn't prove successful for the less attractive girls, but does for the more attractive ones, instructors being human (presumably) like everyone else. But I wonder if the achievement-oriented, intellectually-striving girl usually recognizes that it is her beauty rather than her brains that is bringing about her success. An attractive first-born woman, now a college professor, commented when she heard the results of this study by Dr. Singer, "I'm astonished! I always did exactly as he said. But it never once occurred to me that the instructors weren't responding to my intelligence and zeal. Now I wonder if I haven't been fooling myself all along about any intellectual abilities I might have. Perhaps I have no right to be teaching college students!"

Authorities Suggest Some Practical Applications for the Differences Between First-Born and Later-Born Children

The first-born child has often been described as representing the "past" of society, as compared with the later-born child who is described as being concerned with the practical aspects of present society. It is claimed that the first child tends to carry the past into the present because he adheres to the standards of his parents and these standards come from the past. On the basis of these views, several scholars have made some interesting conjectures about the parts which we might expect first-born and later-born children to play in our society.

Dr. Karl Konig, in a book entitled *Brothers and Sisters*,[22] claims that each individual is destined before birth to fulfill a certain role in society. In order that he may learn the fundamentals of this role, he is caused to be born into a certain place in the family hierarchy. Thus in childhood he has an opportunity to learn the skills he will need in order to carry out his role. The first-born is destined to defend tradition, law, and continuity of customs. He obtains skill in defending these aspects of society as he defends his position when a second child is born into his family. Often, Dr. Konig believes, they take such positions in our society as those of lawyers and judges who are required to defend society against the onslaughts of change. The only child is a first-born whose destiny remains unfulfilled because he is not followed by another child who threatens his position in the family.

Psychoanalyst Irving D. Harris[23] differentiates between first-born and later-born children on the basis of what he believes to be their different intellectual approaches to problems of life and society. The different approaches are developed as the result of different relationships the first-born and the later-born have with their parents. The close relationship of the first-born child with his parents leads to his acquisition of the generalized thinking of the adult. As he experiences the frustration of having sibling competition for the parents, he strives to understand his situation by using general principles. Thus his intellectual approach tends to exhibit a quality that Dr. Harris calls *connectedness*. Later-born children learn their verbal and intellectual approaches through contact with other children. Since children tend to be factual and practical, later-born children remain concerned with the practical details of existence. Their intellectual approaches display a quality which Dr. Harris calls *disconnectedness*.

Dr. Harris finds practical application for his theory in describing the kind of leadership that has been required by the populations of various countries during recent crises. He believes that first sons were needed to be leaders during World War II because they needed to defend that which had been established in the past against hostile forces. They were required to connect the present with the past. Thus first sons Churchill, Hitler, Mussolini, and Franklin Delano Roosevelt were the leaders of their respective countries. Now, Dr. Harris states, the world has developed a need for the practical protectiveness that later sons can give. Thus the leaders in the Western World have been later-borns: Macmillan, DeGaulle, Adenauer and John Kennedy. Dr. Harris points out that the 1960 campaign was the first one in which both candidates (John F. Kennedy and Richard Nixon) were later sons. It is his opinion that a first son (such as Lyndon B. Johnson or John Kennedy's older brother) could not have won that campaign because they could not have met the needs of the population of the United States. In 1964 both candidates, Johnson and Goldwater, were first sons. Of the two, Johnson was in a better position to appeal to the liberal elements of the country which tend to respond to later-born sons. At the same time he held the conservative elements which respond more sensitively to first-borns.

In the 1968 election there were again two main candidates who were later-born. Both Hubert Humphrey and Richard Nixon were second children and second sons in their families. Could it be that those responsible for nominating the candidates were unconsciously selecting persons who could be expected to be more successful than first-borns in solving practical problems? Would it be reasonable to say that Richard Nixon won the election because he tended to be more pragmatic in his general approach? Is it possible that the close final count was somehow due to the similarity between candidates in birth order, so that the concerned voters found it difficult to select between them?

If Dr. Harris is on the right track, political leaders should take heed. It might be advisable for them to evaluate the wishes and needs of society, at the time of any election, and nominate a person whose birth order would be suitable. If current conditions call for someone who will integrate policies and support tradition, a first-born son might be preferable. If practical problems are to be met, a later-born son might be more likely to be elected to the presidency of the United States.

REFERENCES

1. LASKO, JOAN K.: Parent behavior toward first and second children. *Genet Psychol Monogr, 49:*97-137, 1954.
2. PALMER, ROBERT D.: Birth order and identification. *J Consult Psychol, 30:*129-135, 1966.
3. SAMPSON, EDWARD E.: The study of ordinal position: antecedents and outcomes. In Brendon A. Maher (Ed.) : *Prog Exp Personality Res.* New York, Academic Press, 1965.
4. HALL, EVERETTE, and BARGER, BEN: Attitudinal structures of older and younger siblings. *J Individ Psychol, 20:*59-68, 1964.
5. SCHACHTER, STANLEY: *The Psychology of Affiliation.* Stanford, Stanford U Pr, 1959.
6. ARROWOOD, A. JOHN, and AMOROSO, DONALD M.: Social comparison and ordinal position. *J Personality Soc Psychol, 2:*101-104, 1965.
7. WUEBBEN, PAUL L.: Honesty of subjects and birth order. *J Personality Soc Psychol, 5:*350-352, 1967.
8. KAYTON, LAWRENCE, and BORGE, GEORGE F.: Birth order and the obsessive-compulsive character. *Arch Gen Psychiat, 17:*751-754, 1967.
9. ALTUS, WILLIAM D.: Birth order and scholastic aptitude. *J Consult Psychol, 29:*202-205, 1965.
10. OBERLANDER, MARK, and JENKIN, NOEL: Birth order and academic achievement. *J Individ Psychol, 23:*103-109, 1967.
11. ALTUS, WILLIAM D.: Some birth-order parameters related to verbal and quantitative aptitude for 1,120 college students with one sibling. *Amer Psychol, 18:*361, 1963.
12. ALTUS, WILLIAM D.: Birth order and academic primogeniture. *J Personality Soc Psychol, 2:*872-876, 1965.

13. WARREN, JONATHAN R.: Birth order and social behavior. *Psychol Bull, 65*:38-49, 1966.
14. COBB, SIDNEY, and FRENCH, JOHN R., JR.: Birth order among medical students. *JAMA, 195*:312-313, 1966.
15. ALTUS, WILLIAM D.: Birth order and its sequelae. *Science, 151*:44-49, 1965.
16. SAMPSON, EDWARD E.: Birth order, need achievement, and conformity. *J Abnor Soc Psychol, 64*:155-159, 1962.
17. CAPRA, P. C., and DITTES, J. E.: Birth order as a selective factor among volunteer subjects. *J Abnor Soc Psychol, 64*:302, 1962.
18. SUEDFELD, PETER: Birth order of volunteers for sensory deprivation. *J Abnor Soc Psychol, 68*:195-196, 1964.
19. SISHA, JAI B.: Birth order and sex difference in need-achievement and need-affiliation. *J Psychol Res, 11*:22-27, 1967.
20. SINGER, JEROME E.: The use of manipulative strategies: Machiavellianism and attractiveness. *Sociometry, 27*:128-150, 1964.
21. SINGER, JEROME E., and LAMB, PATRICIA F.: Social concern, body size, and birth order. *J Soc Psychol, 68*:143-151, 1966.
22. KONIG, KARL: *Brothers and Sisters*. Blauvelt, St. George Books, 1963.
23. HARRIS, IRVING D., M. D.: *The Promised Seed*. New York, Free Press, 1964.

Chapter V

THE TWO-CHILD FAMILY:
GENERAL CONSIDERATIONS

THE two-child family is a clear-cut case of first-born child and later-born child. For this reason many investigators have used it as the basis for studies of the effect of birth order on the individual. The results of their research suggest that the two-child family may have special characteristics which differentiate it from families with other numbers of children.

California women were recently reported[1] to consider two children an ideal number for a family while their Eastern sisters were reported to prefer four children. For the California woman and for many other women a two-child family may seem to put a reasonable limitation upon family resources of energy and finances but at the same time to offer a means of avoiding the condition of "only child, no child," as the old saying goes. The California woman has been observed to be interested not only in obtaining the good things of life for her children, but also in seeing that her husband and she live comfortable lives. These interests may be hedonistic but they are also realistic. Large families require large homes and ample play space if the members of the families are to be comfortable. Property taxes, costs of maintaining large homes and lack of household help are probably some of the reasons the California woman is interested in limiting the size of her family.

What are other advantages and disadvantages which may follow from having more than one child and less than three children?

The economic advantage for the parents has been mentioned. And it may be that this is the one advantage that we can point out! The four members of the two-child family (parents and children) suffer, in full strength, the impact of two powerful drives on the part of the children: the striving of each to have first place in the affections and attentions of the parents, and the striving of each child to outdo the other in all areas. The parents tend to be more involved with only two children than they are with each of a larger number of children. They may be under considerable emotional tension a great deal of the time because the rivalry between two children seems to stimulate more bickering and quarreling than occurs in families of other sizes.

The children, it is true, escape the loneliness which the only child often experiences. They learn during their nursery years to make some adjustments in terms of the needs of other peers. If they are of different sexes, they become used to members of the opposite sex and, as we shall see, this may give each of them some advantage over the only child in their adult adjustment to sex and marriage. During their growing-up years they have the usual advantage of having a sibling to bring home more information about the outside world than each could acquire alone. Rivalry and occasional help may serve as a desirable stimulus for each of them in developing capacities. Some evidence[2] suggests that they may learn more adequate social adjustment than the only child who has been found to tend toward more acts of delinquency than the child with one sibling.

Parents are often bewildered by the differences between their two children who, on the basis of similar heredity and environment, might be expected to be much alike. But instead these parents sometimes say that they feel as though they are raising two "only" children. The differences they described are usually in a direction indicated by a correspondent who asked the columnist "Dear Abby": "Why is it that the second child is always better adjusted, emotionally, than the first?" "Dear Abby" picked up the *always* and said that the "question assumes something that is not necessarily true."[3] And "Dear Abby" is right; it is not necessarily true. But it does occur often enough that we might well be startled at the consistency of the pattern.

Let us look at the usual course of events in the family with two children. Two parents have one child, a girl or a boy, who is the only child for a period of time which may vary for a year or so to as many as twenty years. That first child has the usual belief about his parents that any only child has: he is sole owner of those parents. His parents have received him with more joy and anxiety than they are likely to feel with the birth of a later child. He has their attention, their interest, their devotion. He need not share these with anyone nor does he need to share his crib, his room, his toys with anyone else. He is, as so often has been said, a kind of monarch in this domestic kingdom.

Why then should he not react in some strong ways to the intrusion of a new baby who is not only given half the "kingdom" that was formerly his, but who is also permitted, as more helpless, to utilize the larger part of the time and attention of the parents?

Sophisticated parents of today "prepare" the first child for the advent of the second. They tell him about the impending arrival of a brother or sister. He is allowed to feel the movement of the baby inside the abdomen of his mother. His parents do all they can to help him accept the new child. Lovingly, they try to bring their first child to a point where he will not feel jealousy or discomfort. But most parents are more or less disappointed with the way things work out. The first child almost always evidences some jealousy. It would seem that some degree of jealousy is perhaps normal under the circumstances. Certainly it has tended to be present no matter how well the child is prepared for the advent of the second.

The blow seems usually to be felt most intensely by the first child when he has been an only child for eighteen months to four years.[4] The impact seems to be less severe if the first child is less than eighteen months old when the second child is born. He is then less aware of the difference made in his life by the second child, and, perhaps, he has not had time to recognize how comfortable he can be all alone in his little "kingdom." At six or seven years of age he is still likely to display some jealousy and hostility. After six or seven years of age and depending somewhat on the level of intelligence of the child, his expression of jealousy may change its form. During earlier years, the expression may be quite direct: open anger, physical aggression such as hitting the younger child. After six years of age, the child may react by acting as though the second child is a kind of toy to be ignored or played with as the older child wishes. Jealousy has been found to occur as a problem with children as old as sixteen years of age. The adolescent first child of fourteen to twenty years of age may often have a special reason to resent the advent of a second child. For many reasons, mothers who have a second child after such a long period of time may give their first child a great deal of responsibility for caring for the baby. Although an adolescent only child will often express great interest in a new baby before it actually arrives, baby sitting duties usually are resented. A sixteen-year-old girl was made almost completely responsible for an infant brother because her mother suffered an injury which incapacitated her for a long time. The daughter became extremely resentful of interference to her school and social activities caused by baby-sitting. Upon graduation from high school, she preferred to take a job which would enable her to live away from home rather than attend college and live at home. When she married a man several years younger than she, she seemed to use him as an outlet for the resentment she had felt toward her younger brother who had caused so much discomfort. She was critical and disdainful toward her husband. He, in turn, was passive and subservient which helped to keep the marriage intact but allowed neither one development as a mature human being.

The jealousy and bewilderment felt by the first child causes him to act in irritable and irritating ways. Often he increases demands for the time and attention of his parents. We will be only fair to this first child if we point out that his parents often press him to decrease requirements for help and attention because they are so involved with the new infant. They are often impatient with him even though he is only continuing a pattern of dependency that they formerly took for granted and may even have found charming. The older child may sometimes horrify them by making over physical approaches toward the "baby" that are hostile and aggressive in nature. Their formerly sweet little first child suddenly seems like some kind of monstrous "bad seed."

Usually, however, the first child learns quickly enough that he had better suppress direct expression of his destructive wishes, particularly when the parents are present. One young mother told me triumphantly that her older boy had completely and sweetly accepted his new baby brother. A week later she reported that she had listened carefully to a little song that she found him crooning over the baby's bassinet. It went: "Goin' to put him down the toy-yet; goin' to put him down the toy-yet."

When parents in the Guatemalan Indian Village of San Pedro la Laguna have similar reason to believe that an older child might "eat the soul" of his sibling, they appeal to the village shaman to help them out, according to investigator Benjamin D. Paul.[5] A ritual is followed in which a young chicken is beaten to death on the back of the older child and the older child is made to eat the maltreated chicken. Thus there is symbolic punishment and appeasement which is considered to alleviate the dangers of the situation for all concerned.

In our country and in most relatively complicated cultural groups, there is no such simple ritual to take care of the matter of sibling jealousy and hostility. The usual reaction of parents is to protect the second and younger child and to feel angry with the first child. They tend to think that "something is wrong" with the first child because he behaves as he does. Their unfavorable reactions confirm the first child's feeling that the very existence of the second child is a threat to his status and happiness. He becomes more angry and hostile, although physical aggression may give way to verbal aggression expressed in quarreling. As time goes on the second child seems to catch onto the fact that the parents will give him their attention when the first child "bugs" him. So, although he may often seem to the parents to scream a little louder than necessary, he tends to withhold direct aggression toward the older child and waits for the parents to punish the older child for him. So he seems to the parents to be quieter, more comfortable to live with than the first child. And the parents consider him to be "better adjusted."

The older child strives in ways other than direct expression of hostility to deal with the threat to his status that is made by the infant intruder. One way of meeting the situation is to "regress:" to return to earlier, more babyish ways of behaving. A year old boy had been well onto learning the skill of walking when a baby sister was brought home in the arms of mother. The boy immediately stopped his progress in walking and had to be carried by his tired and puzzled parents who found themselves with two "babes in arms." He further stopped eating solid foods and accepted only a bottle. Six months passed before he resumed development of more mature ways.

Usually regression to earlier infantile stages meets with little real success. The first child is usually older when the second is born and basic skills of walking, talking, and eating have been established. Returning to babyhood may mean whining and crying more than before or asking for more assistance and attention than formerly seemed necessary. Parents tend to make it quite clear that they do not feel happy about such regression. So the tendency of the child is then to move in a direction which does meet with some success. He intensifies his attempts to be like his parents, to identify with them. He adopts some of their "parental" ways of behaving toward his younger sibling. He sees his parents as authoritative, as being "in charge" and "directive," and so he becomes. Only sometimes parents describe his behavior as "bossy." Continuing to be more and more like his parents, he tends to take over their values, their standards and their morals. After a while he may even adopt a parental role in relating to the parents. They may then complain that he is presumptuous, disrespectful, and disobedient. Sometimes he becomes rebellious toward their authority or even competitive with them as authorities in the family.

The second child, in a family with more than two children, undergoes some of the feelings when a third child is born that the first child had when he was born. But in the two-child family, the second child tends to hold onto the position of being the "unaggressive" one in contrast to the older sibling. He remains the "smaller and younger one." He has no reason to emphasize identification with the "parental" and authoritarian aspects of his parents; to grow up rapidly. Generally he seems less tense and anxious than his older sibling and his parents describe him as more comfortable to live with than the older child.

This pattern of differences between the first child and the second child in the two-child family has been described in various studies. First children are described as having personalities that differ noticeably from those of the second children in the same families. At Harvard, two generations were asked to evaluate first and second children in their families, and the same general pattern was reported by the parents of each generation. The first child was reported to be more commonly adult-oriented, sensitive, serious, conscientious, fearful and studious. Second children were described as showing easy-going friendliness, and to be cheerful, placid, and not studious.[6]

"Dear Abby" told her correspondent that whenever the second child is better adjusted than the first, it might be because the mother has learned something from her first child. In the Harvard study, differences in ways of treating the children that might come out of experience seemed to have no distinguishable effect on the pattern between the children. No differences were found that seemed to be related to the way infants were fed, the date of weaning, dates of toilet training, presence or duration of thumb-sucking, or customary method of punishment. With variations in these conditions, the first-child personality remained the same and the second-child personality remained the same! This does not mean that mothers had not learned something from their first children; it only suggests that what they had learned may not be reflected in what they describe as being "more relaxed" with a second child. It is my belief that the tendency of the first child to identify with the parent, and with the strictest part of the parent's personality, is what makes the difference. And that the differences we see because of the sex of the two children, i.e., whether the family is composed of two boys or two girls or of both sexes, develop out of rather different identifications with the female parent or the male parent. But more about that later.

Professor Emeritus Helen L. Koch found first-born children, in two-child families, to recover less readily from upsets and anger than second-borns and that first-born children evidenced more self-confidence.[7] This finding by another expert is again in the direction of the pattern previously described.

During early years the second child seems to have an advantage over the first as far as general development is concerned. His parents, as we have said, usually describe him as more spontaneous and easier to get along with. Five and six year old second-born children have been found to excel over first-borns on such scales as the Primary Mental Abilities Test. Japanese investigators Abe, Tsuji, and Suzuki[8] found that the score for second-born children on the Draw-a-Man Test was significantly superior to that of first-born children when both were tested at the same age, within ten days of their third birthdays. These were comparisons of the productions of children from the same families. The Draw-a-Man Test offers validity as a test of both intelligence and of the maturity of perception of other people. The higher scores of the second children seemed, at least partially, due to the existence of an older sibling, because the closer the second-born was in age to the older child, the more likely his score was to be higher than that of his sibling. This suggests that he was evidencing the advantage of learning from a first child through the closer association of children near the same ages.

Up to this point we have been examining the differences between the two children in the two-child family while both children are still quite young. Let us now turn to studies and observation of these children when they have had an opportunity to grow somewhat older. We may find some cause for surprise in our new findings!

Dr. Rita Vuyk,[9] of Amsterdam, studied 434 two-child families. The pattern between the two children was similar to the one described above, the older child being less vivacious and less spontaneous than the younger child and more serious and calm. Then three years later she repeated the study with the same families. In general, the same pattern appeared, but with an important difference. When there was a change in the pattern, it was in the direction of relatively favorable development of the older child and relatively unfavorable development of the younger child.

In a study in Scotland,[10] the scores of older siblings on an intelligence scale were compared with the scores of their younger siblings. All of these children were tested at age eleven. The average intelligence of the older siblings was found to be higher than that of the younger siblings.

In London, Mary Stewart[11] found that the elder of two children was more successful than the younger in obtaining grammar school places. First-born children remained longer in school and were represented in greater numbers in such organizations as scouts, guides, and other childrens' uniformed groups.

Two investigators at Bowling Green State University, Dr. B. C. Rosenberg and Dr. B. Sutton-Smith,[12] found first-born students to be superior to second-born in cognitive ability.

Dr. William D. Altus of the University of California at Santa Barbara has made many studies comparing the aptitudes and college attendance of first-born and second-born children in two-child families. He not only found that first-borns demonstrate superior ity to second-borns in verbal aptitude, but that this superiority is so consistent that he could differentiate between first-born and second-born children to a significant degree by using their scores on a test of verbal aptitude.[13]

The same investigator found that, among students coming from two-child families and entering the University from 1960 to 1963, two-thirds were older children.[14]

It now begins to appear that the positions of advantage and disadvantage of the older and younger children in two-child families may shift somewhat as the children become older, at least as far as their educational achievement is concerned.

What may be the reasons for a change in adjustment as the children get older? Dr. Alfred Adler described the second child as usually being in a better position as a child than the first. Not only is he stimulated to effort by a pacemaker, but the first child hastens trouble for himself by fighting, envy, and jealousy. But Dr. Adler said that the younger child may react to inability to compete with his older sibling by escaping "to the useless side of life." He may begin to be lax in his behavior, to lie and to steal; to pave the way toward neurosis, crime and self-destruction. The worst position that the second child can be in, according to Dr. Adler, is to have an older sibling who is brilliant.[15] We can assume that any other condition that would accentuate the impossibility of competition would be equally devastating to a second child.

It seems to me that an important basis for the difference between the two children in later childhood and adulthood might have to do with the difference in opportunity to develop a close early identification with parents. The older child had the parents to himself for a time; he was later able to use them as a direct model for "parental" behavior and he was able to practice this behavior on a younger member of the family. The younger child does not have the experience of feeling stronger than another family member. His tendency is to take advantage of his role as "baby" in the family and he may remain relatively immature and passive. Though this makes him more comfortable for the parents to live with, he does not develop the aggressiveness and independence that his older sibling often does.

Even in childhood, when things go wrong with the second child they may go very wrong. Dr. A. E. Fischer[16] studied twenty-six families in which the behavior of the second-born child was difficult. He found that in nineteen of these families the second-born child began to show symptoms of unhappiness between one and three years of age. There were regressive symptoms such as slowing in speech development, poor eating and sleeping habits, resistance to bladder training and severe crying spells. Still another frequent symptom seems typically that of the younger child as we have described his tendencies: he exhibited excessive quietness. In Dr. Fischer's opinion the second child's troubles grew out of a condition that existed before he was born: his mother's insecurity about being able to care adequately for her *first* child. She showed this insecurity by being oversolicitous in her behavior toward that first child. When the second child is born and exhibits the usual greater tranquillity of any second child, the mother uses this as a rationalization for giving still more attention to her first child. As a result, the second child begins to feel neglected and competitive and reacts in the manner described above.

I have observed the same course of maternal behavior and child reactions to it. Usually such mothers have been women who are intelligent and sensitive and with special reasons for anxiety about their ability to raise children adequately. In one case, a woman had aborted five times before she carried a child to normal birth. She had an intense fear that that first child's every breath might be his last. In another case, the mother had been raised as an only child. She married at an early age, but was not at all eager or ready to have the baby she soon had. In her fear that she might neglect the child because of the resentment she felt about having to take responsibility for him, she went to the opposite extreme of being over-solicitous. The baby soon developed many complicated allergic conditions which further demanded her attention. When the second child was born, a fat and tranquil little girl, the mother left her much to her own baby devices. Soon, however, the girl began to suck her thumb and have long, hard crying spells. She did not begin to speak until she was two years old, and her speech development was slow and immature. Needless to say, it was the second child who became a patient in a psychological clinic.

Fortunately such a degree of pathological development is relatively infrequent. Instead we find that the two children in the two-child family develop within normal limits along the lines of the pattern we have described. The personality difference is that of greater aggressiveness and conscientiousness on the part of the older child and relatively less tension on the part of the younger. The older child is likely to develop stronger intellectual interests and verbal aptitudes than his younger sibling.

We have described evidence of the intellectual differences in approach to later childhood, adolescence, and young adulthood. The personality differences we have described have been found at these later ages.

On the basis of a study of fifty-two pairs of male siblings from two-child families, Dr. Everette Hall and Dr. Ben Barger,[17] at the University of Florida, concluded that the younger and older brothers in their sample seemed "to be different kinds of people." They found the general approach of the older siblings to be serious and possibly dictated by "conscience and a striving for achievement." When asked to reveal what they considered to be "the most important thing in life," they responded with answers which suggested religious values or a philosophy of life. The younger siblings displayed a wide variety of interests which they seemed to value for hedonistic rather than idealistic reasons.

The older siblings seemed to prefer activities which involved people as part of a pattern of organization and control. Younger siblings preferred activities which could be enjoyed for their own sake, such as athletics, and which involved other people as fellow participants or companions.

We may interpret these results as displaying, in part at least, differences in identification with parental standards and behavior. A "parent within" seems to dominate the behavior of the older child; a more relaxed "child within" may determine much of the behavior of the younger sibling.

These results suggest to us that even in adulthood the second child may be more comfortable with himself and with other people than the first child is. The older child as an adult may still be controlling and anxious about achievement. He may achieve more than his younger sibling along lines considered important by society, but he may not have as much fun!

REFERENCES

1. *Ladies' Home Journal:* The California woman. July 1967, p. 63.
2. PARSLEY, M.: The delinquent girl in Chicago: the influence of ordinal position and size of family. *Smith College Studies in Social Work, 3:*274-284, 1933.
3. VAN BUREN, ABIGAIL: Dear Abby. *Los Angles Times,* 1968.
4. KOCH, HELEN L.: Attitudes of young children toward their peers as related to certain characteristics of their siblings. *Psychol Monogr, 70:* No. 426, 1956.
5. PAUL, BENJAMIN D.: Symbolic sibling rivalry in a Guatemalan Indian village. *Amer J Anthropol, 52:*205-218, 1950.
6. MCARTHUR, C.: Personalities of first and second children. *Psychiatry, 19:*47-54, 1956.
7. KOCH, HELEN L.: Some emotional attitudes of the young child in relation to characteristics of his sibling. *Child Development, 27:*393-426, 1956.
8. ABE, K.; TSUJI, K., and SUZUKI, H.: The significance of birth order and age difference between siblings as observed in drawings of prekindergarten children. *Folia Psychiat Neurolo Jap, 17:*315-323, 1964. Abstract in *Psychol Abst,* 1965, No. 4523.
9. VUYK, RITA: Eltern vergleichen ihre beiden kinder zum zweiten mal. (Parents compare their two children for the second time.) *Schweiz. A. Psychol. Anwend., 22:*220-231, 1963. Abstract in *Psychol Abst,* 1964, No. 7935.
10. MAXWELL, J., and PILLINER, A. E. G.: Intellectual resemblance between siblings. *Ann Hu Genet, 24:*23-32, 1960.
11. STEWART, MARY: *The Success of the First Born Child.* London, Workers Educational Association, 1962.
12. ROSENBERG, B. G., and SUTTON-SMITH, B.: Sibling association, family size, and cognitive abilities. *J Genet Psychol, 109:*271-279, 1966.
13. ALTUS, WILLIAM D.: Birth order and mean score on a ten-item aptitude test. *Psychol Rep, 16:*956, 1965.
14. ALTUS, WILLIAM D.: Birth order and academic primogeniture. *J Personality and Soc Psychol, 2:*872-876, 1965.
15. ANSBACHER, HEINZ L., and ANSBACHER, ROWENA R.: *The Individual Psychology of Alfred Adler.* New York, Harper and Row, 1964.
16. FISCHER, A. E.: Sibling relationships with special reference to the problems of the second child. *J Pediat, 40:*254-259, 1952.
17. HALL, EVERETTE, and BARGER, BEN: Attitudinal structures of older and younger siblings. *J Individ Psychol, 20:*59-68, 1964.

Chapter VI

UNDERSTANDING ADULTS AND CHILDREN FROM THE FOUR POSSIBLE KINDS OF TWO-CHILD FAMILIES

IN THE last chapter we described the pattern of differences generally found between the two children in the two-child family. Variations may be found on this main theme which depend on the sex of the children and whether, in the boy and girl family, the boy is older or younger than his sister.

The Boy-Boy Family

When the two children are both boys, their personalities and intellectual approaches tend to follow rather closely the general pattern expected in two-child families. The older boy is likely to exhibit a greater identification with authority and parental values than does his younger sibling. But this does not mean that he is not more in conflict with his parents than is his younger brother. He is likely to seem more serious and to be more tense. He may be more irritable and more irritating. He is likely to be more easily angered. In a Navajo family the older son was named in accordance with this characteristic "Giving out Anger," while his younger brother was called "Gentle Old Man!"[1] While, like all older children of two, he is likely to display superiority in verbal aptitude, he is the only older of two children who has been found superior to the younger in mathematical aptitude, as well as verbal aptitude. This was the case, however, only if his younger brother was close to him in age.[2]

A relatively wide age-span between the two boys seems to be conducive to better adjustment for both of them. Professor Helen L. Koch[3] found that a younger brother tended to display very good social adjustment if he had a brother who was much older than he. Competition between two boys close together in age can be intense, and it is likely to be advantageous in stimulating achievement for the older boy but disadvantageous for the younger boy, who may stop trying. Professor Koch has also found that a boy with an older brother close to him in age is likely to be more withdrawn and dependent than a boy with a much older brother.[4] The older boy is likely to be "parental" in a relatively kind and guiding way.

That the conditions in the boy-boy family may lead to problems is shown by the relatively large number of cases brought to behavior clinics. Such a family seems to contribute more cases to behavior clinics than any other combination of children. One reason for this might be that learning disabilities have been found to occur most frequently with this combination of siblings.[5] Another reason might be that language problems, which can lead to later educational problems, are more frequent among boys in general.[6]

The Girl-Girl Family

Most of the studies to which we have referred have been relationships and situations involving boys. Perhaps there is some connection between the sex of the investigators, who are usually men, and their choice of subjects to study. Perhaps they find it more interesting to look into situations which may throw some light on their own development as children. It is probably only coincidence, but one of the few studies I have been able to find of relationships between sisters was by a woman, Dr. Gertrude M. McFarland.[7]

After careful study of the behavior of twenty-two pairs of sisters, Dr. McFarland concluded that the style of behavior of the child is largely determined by family position. She found distinctive patterns for the behavior of one sister toward the other. Older sisters tended to be more directive, aggressive, helpful and protective toward their younger sisters than their younger sisters were toward them. They showed more rivalry but were also more sympathetic and affectionate toward their younger sisters than their younger sisters were toward them.

As in any other two-child family, the older girl tends toward higher verbal aptitude and achievement than her younger sister.

In contrast with the parents of two boys, the parents of two girls frequently find their older daughter more comfortable to raise than the younger girl. Parents have frequently commented, "My older daughter is just what you want a daughter to be, but my younger daughter is a problem."

What seems to happen in the case of two girls compared with two boys is that the process of identification with the parents is somewhat different.

Like the older boy, the older girl attempts to enhance identification with the parents when the younger child is born. The older boy moves toward closer identification and relationship with his father, but an older girl tends to remain in close contact with her mother. Mother asks her to help in caring for the baby. Her daughter identifies with her; she learns to be like the female and mothering side of her mother. She takes on responsibilities and enjoys being a "good little mother."

Like any other older child, she learns as many ways to be "good" as possible; ways which will be approved by the parents. Unlike the older son, the older daughter usually does not become defiant and rebellious, and so she maintains the support of the parents. Instead of acting out the tensions she feels about retaining the love of her parents as the older boy might, she tends to turn the tension within and to suffer physical ills. In adult life she often has migraine headaches and some instances of alcoholic or drug addiction in the older of two sisters have seemed to result from tension caused by wishes to achieve according to the parents' standards. The alcohol or drugs have been turned to in desperation by women who felt unable to control what seemed to them to be unacceptable impulses, in terms of requirements set up by perfectionistic parents.

The younger of two sisters often finds her paragon of an older sister very hard to take. During the early years she can somewhat compete by being "cute." But after a few years her parents begin to tire of her "babyish" ways and to put pressure on her to "grow up." Meanwhile older sister is bringing home good grades. After a few years she brings boys home. Younger sister watches all this with envy. Because of her relatively young age she can never catch up in skills except in unusual cases. Often during early adolescence she tries to use precocious sexual behavior as a way of competing with or at least catching up with her sister, and her parents view this development with dismay. Since she has not been in a position to acquire the conscience or "parent within" that determines her sister's standards, the younger daughter may move even more toward the "useless side of life" and become involved in delinquency and other anti-social behavior.

She may become quite defiant in the relationship with her parents[8] in contrast with the second son who usually remains reasonably compliant. She may give up scholastic competition with her sister and she seems to be somewhat less likely to achieve a high occupational level than her sister. Although girls are less likely than boys to be taken to clinics for behavior problems, younger sister has been found more frequently to become a patient than her older sister.[9]

As we might expect on the basis of these observations, the younger sister tends to be more variable in her emotional expression than is her older sister. This may be one reason she has been found to express more interest in drama participation in high school and college than her older sister does. She has also been judged the superior of the two in acting ability.[10]

The Two-Child Family With a Representative of Each Sex

Since I am a sister myself, I am sorry to have to say this, but having a sister may work some disadvantage for any other sibling in a two-child family including a girl!

A girl with a sister has been found to be more defiant and less conforming than a girl with a brother.[8] Either girls or boys with brothers have been shown to have consistently higher mathematical aptitude than boys or girls with sisters.[11]

Although the influence of a brother may have a greater effect on the development of a sister than the presence of a sister has on a brother, the presence of a sister may be constructive in decreasing learning problems since these occur in largest number in the boy-only family. It would seem that girls may bring verbal facility into the home while boys tend to add mathematical ability.

Both boys and girls with sisters have been found to be more

emotionally sensitive than boys or girls with brothers.[12] As mentioned in a previous chapter, the presence of a sibling of the opposite sex in a family of any size has seemed to be conducive to relatively early acceptance and understanding of the opposite sex. Clinical evidence suggests that the individual, whose sibling was of the opposite sex, may be more easy about relations with the opposite sex before marriage and may even be more comfortable with the partner during marriage.

The Girl-Boy Family

In the family consisting of two girls, the birth of the younger sister seems to influence the older girl toward greater identification with her mother. The general mode of adjustment seems to be somewhat different when the second child is a boy. Older sister often reacts as though she finds a brother to be more of a challenge to her status than a sister would have been. She may evidence resentment in her attitude toward her mother and she often increases her contacts with her father, seeming to seek more acceptance and companionship with him than with her mother.

One reason for older sister's reaction in this way to the birth of a brother may be that mothers often feel a special pride after they have produced a son. Older daughter is likely to sense what her mother really feels no matter how much mother tries to hide it, and she may fear that her mother will prefer the brother. Consequently she turns for reassurance, and perhaps as a way of punishing her mother, to her father.

Although the situation does not usually reach the point of causing severe disturbance in an older sister, clinics have reported twice as many girls with younger brothers as girls with younger sisters.[9]

Adult females with younger brothers occasionally exhibit a thorough dislike for assuming a feminine role in society. They tend to obtain more years of education than their younger brothers do and more than they would if their sibling were a younger sister.[13]

They may show, in their behavior, attempts to compete with males, and they may say they are "proud of being a woman in a man's world" when they have achieved a place in an occupational field that is usually left mainly to males. Older sister is especially likely to react in this way if she was an only child for four or more years. She then seems to express resentment toward her mother for having produced a masculine rival, by disliking all that is feminine and hence representative of her mother. She further rejects her mother and all that she stands for by moving toward identification with her father. She establishes a position for competition with the new brother by becoming "masculine" before he can compete as a male.

In adulthood she may deny the need to be dependent on a male, and she may accept only relatively passive males as lovers or husband. Sometimes she obviously repeats the childhood sibling pattern by serious involvements with males who are younger than she and who usually can be dominated by her.

However, such inclinations will usually be kept within normal limits. She may only display mild tendencies toward being relatively less feminine and gentle than the usual womanly pattern. What might be a great challenge to her adjustment would be marriage to a man who would bring out her latent identification with the more masculine traits of her father. She is most likely to be comfortable in a marriage if her spouse is an older or oldest brother who is, preferably, four or more years older than she. She would then be likely to relate to him more as the relatively submissive and admiring daughter than as a competitive and dominating older sister. If she marries a younger or youngest brother, she may attempt to dominate and control him.

As we have seen, younger brother seems to offer some problems in adjustment for his older sister. She, in turn, may bring about some problems for him, particularly in the area of full development of masculinity.

The problems of the younger brother of a sister are likely to be the silent, more or less hidden reactions of the younger child in any position. Thus his parents may not be conscious that he is undergoing any maladaptive development. They are likely to be quite comfortable with him, even though he is experiencing two conditions which may be threatening to him as a male; as a younger child in the family he tends toward relative passivity and this tendency may be accentuated by aggressive competitiveness on the part of older sister.

Usually the circumstances in the family are such that he learns to express his masculine aggression and does not allow his sister to dominate him. Whenever serious problems arise, it has usually been observed that relationships between the members of the family are disturbed in a number of ways.

It is a disadvantage to the younger brother of a sister to be too much the favorite of his mother. In such cases we often find that his father is either indifferent or openly hostile to him and that the boy may spend a great proportion of his time in the company of his mother. He then tends to identify with his mother rather than with his father. Since, through the sibling relationship, he is also thrown into much contact with his sister, his masculine identification is further threatened because she is a feminine model in addition to his mother's feminine model. Although we have no evidence that this is so, there may be cause in extreme cases to consider the possibility of a homosexual adjustment.

In adulthood the younger brother of a sister sometimes seems to be relatively passive and to be less strongly masculine than he might be. Often he seems to add to what might be a problem, a further challenge to his adjustment, by marrying a woman who is dominating and controlling. Often, then, difficulties with the spouse will lead him to turn to his older sister for comfort, and she will assume a strong maternal role with him which will infuriate his wife and cause further marital trouble.

The wives of these men will often complain that their husbands are not sufficiently aggressive. Often, although they may know little about business or professional matters, they will influence greatly the judgments of their husbands even in such matters. It is apparent, of course, that wife and husband in such a marriage have assumed roles as "older sister and younger brother."

The girl friend or wife of the younger brother from the mixed-sex, two-child family apparently should be a woman who is neither completely dependent in practical matters, nor so emotionally aggressive that she challenges her partner's masculine identification. The male who was raised in the younger sibling position sometimes tends to be uncertain of his ability to assume financial responsibility for a household. In fact, like many younger children, he may prefer not to be tied down by such mundane matters. But, since he is a male, he resents consciously or unconsciously, any implication by his wife that this makes him less a

man than other men. With adequate emotional support, acceptance, faith in his abilities, he is an able husband and father, with
the added advantage of being variable enough never to be boring.

The Boy-Girl Family

This sibling situation seems to be a rather comfortable one,
with special advantages for the older child, the male.

Often the mother of such a family continues to give the first
child special attention and interest despite the birth of a second
child. She tends to feel special pride in having produced a male
child. She tends to place less responsibility for the everyday household tasks on a son after a baby is born, than she does on a daughter who is first in the family. Her first child, then, moves toward
identification with his father, but he does it more naturally and
without as much hostility toward mother as an oldest girl child
does.

Although he usually does not feel as intensely competitive with
a sister as he does with a younger brother, he still makes sure that
his status is retained by emphasizing his masculinity in contrast to
her femininity. As he grows older he is likely to develop what almost amounts to disdain of feminine interests and activities. His
wife may complain that he is unwilling to understand her "feminine weaknesses," such as the queasiness of pregnancy and the ex-
hausting physical effort of caring for small children. One male
raised in such a childhood role considered it taken for granted that
his wife should mow the lawn, complete the gardening, and wash
the cars once a week. He was nonplussed when she refused to help
him build a garden wall by hauling the bricks to him in a wheel-
barrow. A woman should get over those "little sister" limitations!

Often the male raised in such a role expects his wife to give him
a great deal of service in everyday matters of serving meals, care of
clothing and taking care of his correspondence. It is not for him to
take on feminine tasks.

The intensity of his adherence to such differentiation between
the roles and responsibilities of the sexes may be in direct relation
to the number of years of age between himself and his younger
sister. If he is two or less years older than she, it is very likely
that they were relatively often playmates in childhood and that he
developed some feminine interests.[14]

The younger sister of a brother may like him rather well and she may be rather proud of him. She is especially likely to feel this way about him if she is certain that her mother is as fond of her daughter as she is of her son. Younger sister is glad to have father's love and appreciation, but father's attitude is not as important to her as is that of her mother.

One of the ways Mother demonstrates her regard for her daughter is by giving her just as much time and attention after early infancy as older brother receives. Since girls tend to be relatively more quiet than boys and second children in any case can be expected to be more relaxed and self-contained, mother may turn a great deal of her attention to an active older brother. Eventually this may result in the small girl's developing ways of behaving that will bring attention from mother, and the behavior will be selected on the theory that any attention, even annoyed attention, is better than none at all. Younger sisters have been observed to change from pleasant passivity during the first year or two of babyhood to active annoying aggressive behavior. Such tactics as fighting, getting hurt and breaking things have kept mother both interested and angry. One girl moved from an irritating pattern during early childhood to an adolescent stance of constantly embarrassing her mother in front of other people or doing almost anything insolent or rude that would keep her mother's attention on her.

Younger sisters of brothers are also often resentful of what they consider the unfairness of having to help with household tasks, while older brothers are usually absolved from these duties, mainly because they do not seem to fit his male role. In many cases these younger sisters may become very hostile toward their older brothers and defiant toward the parents, who require what seems to her an unfair portion of the household responsibilities. It is important that the sons be given their fair share of such duties, and it is usually possible to divide up the work which the children may do in terms of more "masculine" or more "feminine" tasks. It is possible, too, to arrange matters so that both children have an equal number of tasks to be done daily, a matter that is of some importance. Household tasks tend to require everyday attention; more "masculine" tasks often do not. This gives the impression to the girl-child that she is the only one of the two to work everyday in helping her parents. If the younger sister of a brother is required to do things for him, such as taking care of his room or washing his clothes for him, it is only the most unusual of parents who can keep the situation from reaching anarchy!

Younger sisters of brothers tend to develop a strong adult identification with their mothers and with the feminine side of things in general. This identification includes a preference for the roles of mother and housewife despite their childhood complaints about having to help with household tasks. Their identification is usually most clearly shown when they marry. They tend to become very housewifely and to throw themselves with gusto into cooking and cleaning and raising their young.

The combination of the usual passivity of the younger child and the strong feminine identification of the younger sister of a brother makes it difficult in many cases for her to get started on a career unless an early marriage solves her problem. She is likely to have little drive toward becoming proficient in a business or professional career unless economic circumstances force her into one.

REFERENCES

1. DYK, WALTER: *Son of Old Man Hat.* Lincoln, U Nebraska Pr, 1938, p. 187.
2. ALTUS, WILLIAM D.: Some birth-order parameters related to verbal and quantitative aptitude for 1,120 college students with one sibling. *Amer Psychol, 18:*361, 1963.
3. KOCH, HELEN L.: Der einfluss der geschwister suf die personlichkeitsentwicklung jungerer knaben (The influence of siblings on the personality development of younger boys.) *Jb. Psychol. Psychother., 5:*211-225, 1958. Abstract in *Psychol Abst.,* 1961, No. 1107.
4. KOCH, HELEN L.: Attitudes of young children toward their peers as related to certain characteristics of their siblings. *Psychol Monogr, 70:*No. 426, 1956.
5. HODGES, ALLEN, and BALOW, BRUCE: Learning disability in relation to family constellation. *J Ed Res, 55:*41-42, 1961.
6. KOCH, HELEN L.: Sibling influence on children's speech. *J Speech Disorders, 21:*322-328, 1956.
7. McFARLAND, MARGARET B.: *Relationships Between Young Sisters as Revealed in Their Overt Responses.* New York, Columbia U Pr, 1938.

8. SCHMUCK, RICHARD: Sex of sibling, birth order position, and female dispositions to conform in two-child families. *Child Development, 34*:913-918, 1962.

9. LEVY, J.: A quantitative study of behavior problems in relation to family constellation. *Amer J Psychiat, 10*:637-654, 1931.

10. SUTTON-SMITH, BRIAN, and ROSENBERG, B. G.: The dramatic sibling. *Percept Motor Skills, 22*:993-994, 1966.

11. SCHOONOVER, SARAH M.: The relationship of intelligence and achievement to birth order, sex of sibling, and age interval. *J Educ Psychol, 50*:143-146, 1959.

12. ROSENBERG, B. G.; SUTTON-SMITH, B., and GRIFFITHS, JUDITH: Sibling differences in empathic style. *Percep Motor Skills, 21*:811-814, 1965.

13. SMELSER, WILLIAM T., and STEWART, LOUIS H.: Where are the siblings? *Sociometry, 31*:294-303, 1968.

14. KOCH, HELEN L.: Sissiness and tomboyishness in relation to sibling characteristics. *J Genet Psychol, 88*:231-244, 1956.

Chapter VII

THE ONLY CHILD IN CHILDHOOD
OR "IS THERE ANY HOPE?"

THE only child is often somewhat self-conscious about his state. Those of us with brothers and sisters are perhaps a bit more curious about him than we are about people raised in other family positions. The only child seems both to himself and to us to be a bit set off from other people. It is possible that for us, who are not only children, there is a touch of envy increasing our interest. Deep within most of us, buried by childhood repression, is the wish that we might have had our parents all to ourselves; that their affection and energies might always have been directed wholly toward us. The only child, on this basis, might seem to have it made!

In an earlier chapter we examined some of the findings about differences between first and later children in families. It was pointed out that the group of first-born children usually encompassed only children and those other first-borns, the older or oldest children. Since all of these are the first children of their parents, many of their developmental conditions are the same, and hence they are likely to take on similar personality trends in many areas.

However, the only child may also be found to have many experiences and characteristics similar to those of youngest children, since he is the last as well as the first of his family!

Let us now see if we can isolate conditions which are considered to be peculiar to the position of only child.

It is such a usual thing in our society for parents to have more than one child that it is often questioned whether or not parents of an only child might not be different in some ways from other parents. Dr. Alfred Adler claimed that the parents of only children did tend to be different in some ways. He described the only child as being born into a "timid and pessimistic environment."[1] Apparently he assumed that parents of an only child restricted family size because of anxiety about economics. Whatever the fears of the parents might be, statistics suggest that they are likely to be in better economic circumstances than the parents of larger families, and that their social status is, on the whole, higher than average.[2]

Other conditions have been found which are sometimes responsible for family size limitation. Both youngest children and only children have been found to display more congenital defects than first children followed by siblings.[3] In many cases parents probably hesitate to have more children after a child has been born with a defect of some kind, both from a fear that the defect will appear again and from a recognition that available financial resources must be used to help the child they already have.

Physical conditions of mothers may have something to do with family limitation. Mothers of only children have been found to experience more difficult pregnancies than mothers of more than one child.[4]

Fathers, too, have been given responsibility for the limitation of family size. The fathers of only children have been found to have poorer health or to complain of more physical symptoms than the fathers of more children. It has been my observation that the fathers of only children may sometimes be a bit dependent, for emotional or physical reasons, on the attention and care of their wives. In rare instances such a father has become impotent after fathering one child, a means of securing psychological assurance that no more children will arrive.

The parents of any first child are likely to be quite anxious about their ability to care for their child. To these anxieties, the parents of the only child may add special tensions that grow out of conditions such as we have just described. Since no later children arrive to give them more perspective on what they may expect from themselves and from their child, they may place special pressures on their child during all the years he lives in their home.

A source of considerable anxiety for the parents may be the physical health of their youngster, particularly during his early childhood. Since there is no later sibling with whom to share their attention, their one child receives the full force of their anxiety when he has the usual childhood illnesses. As a result of this, the only child is in danger himself of becoming overly sensitive to physical conditions and to carry on both in childhood and adulthood a tendency to allow minor ills to interfere with daily activities. The only child may also learn to use complaints about physical illnesses as a way of avoiding situations which actually distress him emotionally rather than physically. In childhood he may be able to stay home from school if he complains of a stomach upset or a headache. In adulthood the female only child is more likely to use such excuses as ways of avoiding difficult situations than is the male only child.

As is the oldest child, the only child is the recipient of considerable pressure from the parents to behave in a right and proper way. Unlike the oldest child, the only child continues throughout childhood and adolescence to have the same close and undivided attention and control by his parents. The parents of several children have an opportunity to discover that the misbehavior of one of their children does not implicate them as inadequate parents. They can see some success in their role as parents, although it may be sometimes with one child and sometimes with another. But the parents of the only child remain sensitive to the failures or the misbehavior of that one chick. And that one child remains the full target for the expressions of anxiety, dismay and anger by the parents.

Parents tend to discipline their first children more severely than they do their later children.[5] The mother usually is first disciplinarian of all the children, with the father tending to take over discipline of the older children, particularly if they are male, as younger children come along.[6] The only child, however, tends to remain the target for the demands, expectations, and the discipline of both parents. If one or both of the parents is an angry, violent person, this can result in considerable emotional disturbance for the child. An adult male only child has described nightmares filled with terror during all his life, and in adulthood he has often been subject to vague formless feelings of anxiety and fear which interfere with his professional development because they prevent his taking on new responsibilities. Both of his parents were angry, unhappy people who were easily upset by their child. He remembers that when he was a small child he was often kicked by a furious father, and he often ran in terror from a father who was unbuckling his belt to use as a weapon with which to beat him. Often he cowered on his bed protecting his head as his mother rained blows on him. The physical punishment was never so intense that his body was marked; the marks were the invisible ones of emotional disturbance.

Sometimes one or both parents of an only child will resolve that the child is to reach heights of achievement that will realize parental ambitions not achievable by the parent himself. Famous persons who were only children often point out that the first move of their parents is, then, to make sure that their child is not "contaminated" by contact with unsuitable playmates. They will not permit their children to be friendly with neighbors considered to be of lower social, educational, or financial status. As a result these only children experienced extreme loneliness in childhood, and a possible deprivation in the development of their ability to enjoy and achieve relationships with other people. That may have something to do with their adult difficulties in acquiring just an ordinary amount of personal happiness and security. The movie actress Mary Astor[7] tells in her autobiography how her father failed in his own excessive ambitions and then turned his energies toward development of the talents and potentialities of a daughter who seemed to have both unusual musical ability and physical attractiveness. He kept her away from other children, making sure that she learned in what ways he considered them inferior. He trained her as carefully to be a movie actress as any filly is trained to win the Kentucky Derby. When she was in her middle teens, she fulfilled his ambitions and achieved for her parents the financial and social status they wanted, but as soon as she herself was cut loose from the constant direction of her father, she floundered on emotional shoals in relationships with other people. It was years and many tears later before she was able to develop values and attitudes with which she could guide her own behavior.

Perhaps a happier example of the results of pressures of parents to help their one child achieve at high levels is that of our one President who was an only child, Franklin Delano Roosevelt. His wealthy parents poured advantages on him, and his mother supervised his activities most carefully even through years of his presidential dignity.

Only children do not seem to react to the pressures of their parents for achievement with the same tensions that the older or oldest child may display. They may accomplish high levels in professions or occupations, but they seem more motivated by a wish to please someone who is important to them and who is ambitious for them, rather than by any internalized self-requirements for such achievement. They are more comfortable, than the first child followed by siblings, if they do not achieve at a high level. This more relaxed attitude probably occurs because there is no sibling rival to force the only child to make the parents' ambitions and admonitions his own, to internalize them so that he can "out-parent the parents" in competing with the younger brother or sister.

Attempts to find personality differences between only children and children with siblings have met with quite inconsistent results. There is some evidence that the only child, like the oldest child, tends toward more feelings and display of irritability and anger than children in other sibling positions, as described in the chapter comparing all first-born children with later-born children.

Only children have sometimes been found to be more frequently brought to behavior clinics than children from other family positions. When this occurs, it should be considered that the reason is not necessarily greater absolute disturbance on the part of the only child. The situation is such that the parents of the only child, lacking perspective gained through comparison with other children, may be overly sensitive to their only child's behavior. Having no other children, they are also in better economic circumstances to seek help than other parents might be.

Several differences have been consistently observed between the only child and older or oldest children. The only child often seems to be generally more self-confident and relaxed throughout childhood and adulthood than are the other first-born children. He retains the full "ownership" of his parents and never experiences the disappointment of having others take his place. Although he receives the full brunt of the parents' anxieties about his welfare and their adequacy as parents, he is not subject to their demands that he be conforming and parental and to their criticism if he does not meet their standards. Hence he generally feels more confident than the older or oldest child about being able to meet the standards of any authority.

The only child has also been found consistently to feel and display less jealousy than does the older or oldest child.[8] He has never had to give up his place nor his belongings to another child or later children in the family. He does not suffer the severe and painful jealousy that the older or oldest child does with the advent of the next sibling. And throughout childhood and adolescence he is likely always to have and receive more in the way of material things than most of the children he knows. One female only child told me that at Christmas time she would hide some of her presents from other children visiting her, feeling somewhat ashamed that she received so much more than they! But no only child has been found to suffer any serious consequences from such shame, while older or oldest children do seem to carry with them uncomfortable feelings of jealousy because they must both share and often give up some of what they have or want.

There is evidence that the only child may often surpass other children in the intellectual level he exhibits on school scales, and he often receives relatively higher grades in school.[9] One usual explanation of this difference is that the only child tends to come from families with higher socio-economic and educational levels than children from larger families.[2]

Even though there may be some drawbacks in having the complete attention of two parents, the only child receives many advantages as the result of being the one child in the family.

As mentioned before he is usually relatively self-confident. At an early point he comes to view himself as being of considerable importance as an individual because he receives so much special attention. He develops strong and intense attitudes and feelings and usually is quite an individualistic person in adulthood. He is likely to draw the attention of other people and often their admiration because he seems to feel so comfortable being the special kind of person he is likely to feel himself to be.

An advantage often mentioned for the only child is the economic one. He does not have to share the financial resources of the family with other children. Since the cost of a bicycle doesn't have to be doubled or tripled to meet the needs of other children in the family, the only child can have the best one available. A party dress can be the prettiest (and most costly) in the shop because only one must be purchased. In our society, ownership of valuable things tends to give the individual some status. Perhaps this is most true for the adolescent individual in our society who is very conscious of the financial worth of things. Since the only child usually has such things, he obtains some feeling of status and value through such ownership.

Living for a long time as one child with two adults leads the only child to develop a strong self-concept as child. Having viewed himself as a child among adults all during his growing years, he is likely to have some difficulty in changing his self-perception even when he is adult. Since his parents perceive him as a child in relation to themselves, they may be somewhat slow to increase his responsibilities and to require more mature behavior of him as he grows older. So the only child may come to adulthood still feeling and thinking rather like a child. The husband of an only child remarked, "She goes through life like an innocent little fawn!"

We have examined some of the results of being a one child with two adults. What might be some of the advantages and disadvantages for the only child in some of the more complicated areas of human adjustment?

Perhaps one of the most dangerous areas for future emotional adjustment and the source of much subtle disturbance is the child's struggle with his love for the parent of the opposite sex. The child with siblings, even the oldest child, learns that neither parent can be his alone; other children share the love and attention of each parent. But the only child has the parents to himself with no competition with peers. The tendency of any child seems to be to try, during the early years of development, to be first with the parent of the opposite sex, and the only child is likely to have the illusion that this is possible since he has no peer competition. And his parents are likely to react with intensity to his struggles to be first with one of them.

Dr. Sigmund Freud was perhaps the first to describe the "oedipal" situation involving a so-called "love affair" between parent and children. Dr. Freud observed that a child not only looks to his parents for love and has intense love feelings toward them, but he may feel toward the parent of the opposite sex as one who might be his husband or wife. A child with brothers or sisters has the reality of having to share the parents from a very early stage. The only child can have the illusion of completely "owning" his parents. The love for the parent of the opposite sex and the wish to have that parent entirely to oneself has only one challenger. That challenger, however, is a most powerful one: the parent of the opposite sex. The only child tends to become very involved in love and hate feelings for the parents, and it has been said that he may have more difficulty than a child in any other position in coming to accept the true relationship between himself and his parents.[10]

In childhood, there is often the display of much emotional intensity in the relation with the parents. The girl child usually directs greater affection toward the father and the boy child toward the mother. Although the reason for disturbance is not usually consciously understood by the three participants, the child's struggle to obtain the love of the parent of the opposite sex can often make for much emotional strain in the one-child family. The parent of the same sex as the child will find himself unconsciously in competition with his child for the attention and affection of the spouse. Sometimes the rivalry will become out in the open as apparently it did in the family of Mary Astor. She describes how uneasy she felt as a child because her mother seemed to resent the attention and time her father directed toward his daughter in the interests of furthering her career.

It is very difficult—but very important—that the three members of the one-child family should come to strike the proper balance of love and intimacy among themselves.

Sometimes the problem seems to be related to the needs of one or other parent for the companionship and occasionally for the support of the child. Often a mother will turn to her son for the closeness and warmth she may not feel that she is obtaining from her husband. Cases have been known where a mother whose husband was away from home a great deal on business matters has encouraged her son to sleep in her room or even in her bed until his late adolescence "because I am frightened and would like to have your protection." In some clinical cases an only son has allied himself so completely with his mother that he (and she) will see themselves as one family with the father as an outsider largely in opposition to them. It is needless to say, perhaps, that such relationships may result in a homosexual development on the part of the boy. Certainly they make it difficult for him to develop the usual male identification, interests and feelings. Sometimes it is simply the case that the mother is very proud of her son and over-emphasizes interest in his welfare and achievement. She may aid and protect him to such an extent that he becomes a kind of "mamma's boy" who will never be able to feel as close to any other person, including his wife, as he does to his mother.

Often closeness between an only child and a parent will develop to an unhealthy degree because the other parent has been separated from them by divorce or death. A girl only child who grows up in the care only of her mother may develop such a strong combination of dependency on her mother and protectiveness of her mother that she will find it difficult to develop relationships outside the home even during late adolescence and early adulthood.

To go to the opposite extreme, if the parent of the opposite sex is insensitive to the needs of the only child for affection and attention, or is perhaps basically an unaffectionate person, the child may react with great intensity to what he fantasies to be complete rejection. Often violent feelings of hate or anger will develop which the child will direct at the supposedly rejecting parent. Often this anger is not fully directed until the adolescent years of the child, when it will bring about much conflict between the child and the parent of the opposite sex.

The condition which is most conducive to a comfortable working through of these oedipal wishes of the child is that of a warm, mature relationship between the parents. Such a relationship permits them to feel comfortably secure with each other, not competitive with their child, and yet allows them to be tolerant of their child's variable behavior.

Sometimes, however, it happens that the parents of an only child will be so engrossed in the relationship with each other that their child will develop a feeling of being "left out" as a member of the family. This sometimes occurs in a family in which one of the parents is himself or herself an only child who demands constant attention from the spouse. In other cases, one or the other parent may require a great deal of the spouse's care and attention because he is physically ill. Sometimes the mother of an only child will feel relatively free to throw herself into activities outside the home because she is not as engrossed with home duties as would be the mother of a larger family. She may then be more concerned in sharing occupational experiences or social life with her husband than in sharing her time with her child. Consequently only children have frequently had the specific complaint that "Mother never came to P.T.A. meetings" or "Mother didn't come to school when I was in the graduation play because she was needed at the office that day."

The only child who feels very much "left out" of the parental relationship may attempt to establish a close relationship with some other person outside the immediate family circle. An affectionate, interested grandmother may serve this purpose. It may sometimes be a neighbor to whom the child will turn. Sometimes the only child will cause his parents to be concerned because he strikes up a constant companionship with a neighborhood child who is for some reason or other left out of play by other children. Since such a child is often retarded or seems otherwise inadequate, the parents of the only child may be quite distraught about their child's selection of a playmate. The only child is, of course, particularly interested in the child because he is always available for companionship.

It is almost impossible to avoid for the only child all feelings of being "left out" of the relationship between the parents. Important things go on between them in which the child can have no part; there are secrets between them. Decisions are made without consulting the child. It is very important, then, that the parents of an only child make a special effort to include their child in family discussions and plans whenever it is at all suitable to do so. If the only child does not come to feel part of the family activities, he may retain into adulthood a feeling that he is never to be a natural part of any relationship or activity.

The only child often suffers from loneliness more than does a child in any other family position because there is the objective circumstance of having no other children present to offer noise and companionship. When other children are sitting together in their homes watching television and sharing laughter and comments, the only child usually is watching his "very own set" with no quarreling about which program to look at, but also without companionship. Parents of only children tend to spend a great deal of time in their own adult activities, having no younger children to keep them at home. Hedy LaMarr describes herself as an only child as: "alone a great deal. My parents were busy . . ."[11] She claims that her loneliness forced her into fantasy play which later led to her development as an actress. As do many only children, she conjured up fantasy companions and often talked to herself. Only children frequently develop languages of their own which are intelligible only to themselves and to their fantasied companions.

Despite the frequent loneliness of only children, they have been found in some studies to be socially popular and to have outgoing personalities.[2,9]

A well balanced social life seems to require that an individual perceive other children with some degree of clarity. Drawings of prekindergarten children have suggested that firstborn children may not perceive other children as clearly as do the later children.[12] Apparently a child with older siblings who are in close contact with him tends to gain more clear perception of other children than does the child who is mainly in the company of adults. A child will usually draw a picture of a person who is of the same sex as herself and of similar age. When the same child is asked to draw a person of the opposite sex, that drawing is likely to be of a child of similar age. A female only child who had little contact with other children and who was the center of attention of several adults, parents and other relatives, drew first an adult female and then what she described as a "forty-year-old" man. Her interest and understanding were clearly directed toward adults.

It is important for parents of the only child to encourage social participation of their child in activities with other children. It has been mentioned that some parents who are ambitious for their only children may deprive them of the companionship of other children. What may happen if a child does not have the companionship of other children is suggested by an experiment of Dr Harry F. Harlow and Dr. Margaret Kuenne Harlow[13] with two rhesus monkeys, one male and one female. Each was isolated in the exclusive company of his or her mother until the infants had reached the age of seven months. Brought together at that age, they did not play together. The female would use play apparatus, but the male monkey would not leave his mother. Furthermore, the mother would not permit the small female to come near her and her son. Even after they had both been separated from their mothers for two months and would be expected to experience some need for contact, they did not play together.[13]

As both child and adult, only children sometimes evidence a remarkable curiousity about other human beings, as though they are constantly searching for information that will make others and their behavior intelligible to them. The sisters of a man who had married an only child told me that they were constantly astonished at the questions she would ask them about everyday matters they thought everyone understood. "What dress do you think I should wear to that party next week?" she would ask them. Or: "That woman told me thus-and-so. What do you think she meant?" And she would listen to their answers as though she were just learning to be a human being. She was not content with the information she had received from her parents; she wanted advice from *peers*.

In more extreme cases the child may withdraw from social participation. The possibility that this may carry into adulthood is suggested by the fact that in one study of seven hundred schizophrenic patients, the least sociable patients were the only children.[14]

REFERENCES

1. ADLER, ALFRED: *What Life Should Mean to You*. New York, Putnam, 1958, p. 152.
2. BONNEY, M. E.: Relationships between social success, family size, socio-economic home background, and intelligence among school children in grades III to V. *Sociometry, 7*:26-39, 1944.
3. CUSHNA, BRUCE; GREENE, MITCHELL, and SNIDER, BILL C. F.: First born and last born children in a child development clinic. *J Individ Psychol, 20*:179-182, 1964.
4. MAUCE, GEORGES, and RAMBAUD, PAULE: Le rang de l'enfant dans la famille (The child's rank in the family). *Rev Franc Psychianal, 15*:253-260, 1951. Abstract in *Psychol Abst*, 1952, No. 3325.
5. HILTON, IRMA: Differences in the behavior of mothers toward first-

78 *Birth Order and Life Roles*

and later-born children. *J Personality Soc Psychol, 7*:282-290, 1967.

6. HENRY, ANDREW F.: Sibling structure and perception of the disciplinary role of parents. *Sociometry, 20*:67-74, 1957.
7. ASTOR, MARY: *My Story*. New York, Doubleday, 1959.
8. FOSTER, S.: A study of the personality make-up and social setting of fifty jealous children. *Ment Hyg, 11*:53-77, 1927.
9. GUILFORD, R. B., and WORCESTER, A. A.: A comparative study of the only and non-only child. *J Genet Psychol, 38*:411-426, 1930.
10. FENICHEL, OTTO: *The Psychoanalytic Theory of Neurosis*. New York, Norton, 1945.
11. LAMARR, HEDY: *Ecstasy and Me*. New York, Fawcett World, 1966.
12. ABE, K.; TSUJI, K., and SUZUKI, H.: The significance of birth order and age difference between siblings as observed in drawings of prekindergarten children. *Folia Psychiat Neurolo Jap, 17*:315-325, 1964. Abstract in *Psychol Abst*, 1965, No. 4523.
13. HARLOW, HARRY F., and HARLOW, MARGARET KUENNE: Social deprivation in monkeys. *Sci Amer, 207*:136-146, 1962.
14. SCHOOLER, C., and SCARR, S.: Affiliation among chronic schizophrenics: relation to intra-personal and birth order factors. *Personality, 30*:178-192, 1962.

Chapter VIII

THE ONLY CHILD IN ADULTHOOD

NO POSITION in the family constellation necessarily causes the individual to be unhappy or inadequate or somehow objectionable in adulthood. It is, perhaps, more important to emphasize this fact in relation to the only child than to the child or adult from any other family position. Only children are frequently referred to as "spoiled" both by themselves and by other people. And yet any one of us has friends, acquaintances, relatives, who grew up as only children and are living in ways that are purposeful and pleasant. It is difficult to see how the word "spoiled" can be applied to them in any meaningful way.

Only children are likely to do better than the average in their school achievement. Like other first-borns, they tend to make higher grades in secondary school and in college than children coming from other family positions, and they tend to be among those who go on to graduate study.[1] We undoubtedly see the influence of some advantages of having only one child to draw on family resources. The parents can financially support activities which give their child cultural and social experiences and stimulate intellectual development. They usually are in a better position to give that child financial support through the years of advanced education than are the parents of larger families.

Although we have as yet no final evidence of the levels of professional and business achievement to be expected of persons coming from each birth position in the family, the evidence we have suggests that the only child continues his development in the direction of better than average success.

Dr. Alfred Adler states that the only child "forms such a style of life that he will be supported by others and at the same time rule them."[2] The only child learns at an early age to utilize the help and support that his parents can give him, and in adulthood he tends to retain the ability to make use of the help of other people. In his occupational life he often has the great advantage of feeling comfortable and self-confident with adult substitutes for parental domination: the bosses in any work situations. Generally in childhood he learned that he had but to ask and he would receive from his parents, and so he continues to take for granted that authority will give him a good reception.

A disadvantage for some only children, in relying on such help from supposedly stronger people, is that they never come to accept their own capabilities. No matter what the outside world says about his abilities, such an only child will retain an inner feeling that he could not have succeeded through his own efforts, and he will have little enjoyment of his success. Often such only children will also have retained a strong self-concept of being still a child in a world of adults.

The male only child, like any other male first-born in a family, is likely to receive special pressure and encouragement by his parents to achieve along lines that will enhance family status. Nevertheless, the male only child does not seem to acquire a drive for achievement that is as tense and driven as that of many older or oldest children. The older or oldest child not only wishes to conform to his parents' requirements for him, but he also desires to compete with his younger siblings. The only child relies on the advantages given him by others and quite comfortably in most cases moves toward achievement as the result of them. He is glad to please his parents, but often his chief motivation for working is to obtain the good things he can buy and the pleasant situations he can afford as a result of his efforts. Often this relatively relaxed attitude in the work situation is an advantage for him because it enables him to enjoy and be enjoyed by his colleagues.

Dr. Stanley Schachter[3] of Columbia University concluded, from a study of differential responses of college girls to the threat of severe shock, that the only children among them tended to be less apprehensive, anxious, or frightened than other first-born children. In line with this finding, he quoted evidence that only children are more likely than other first-born children to be effective fighter pilots among American jet "aces."

It has recently been reported in *Newsweek*[4] that twenty-one of the twenty-three astronauts who had travelled into space by the end of 1968 were first-born children. The two exceptions were so isolated from siblings by death in one case, and many years difference in age in the other, that even they might be considered essentially first-born. Among these astronauts there was found to be a proportion of only children far beyond that to be expected in the general population. The three astronauts who made the first trip to the moon, during the Christmas season of 1968, were only children. The writer of the report referred to research suggesting that only children may develop more independence, more self-reliance, and more courage than children with siblings because they are so often alone during childhood.

We have as yet no reliable evidence that any occupation might be more suitable for a person from one sibling position than for a person from another position. Yet it is possible that someday we will find this to be the case. The actress Hedy LaMarr tells us in her autobiography that "I don't think I would have been an actress had I not been an only child."[5] It is her opinion that the occupation of acting grew out of the fantasy play that she engaged in as a solitary only child. Dr. Adler might, however, have another opinion because he states that the only child is accustomed to "retaining the center of the stage without effort," and it is more natural to him than to other people to be the center of attention in adulthood.[2] Still another possibility lies in a statement made by actor and creative writer Fred Allen to the effect that the "actor has to remain the child."[6] The self-concept of being a child is often retained in adulthood by the only child and this may form an advantage in a career such as acting.

On the other hand, another condition of development of the only child may point in the direction of his being specifically unsuited for occupations where sensitive interpersonal observation is involved. I am not sure what occupations might be considered to require particular facility in extrasensory perception, but whatever they are the only child might not be the most promising person to take them on! In Great Britain, C. E. Green utilized the readers of two publications to study the extrasensory perception of persons coming from the different sibling positions. Although they conceded that the results did not definitely indicate the existence of such abilities, and that the whole area of evidence for extrasensory perception is still controversial, the readers who were first-born in their families did tend to show more positive signs of the ability than did later-born children. But if a first-born child were also the only child in his family, the results were negative![7] It is possible that there is some relationship between this finding and the only child's relative isolation from peers in childhood, as described in the last chapter. The only child might not have the same opportunity to develop sensitive interpersonal observation, but he might not have the same need as the older or oldest child to use cues to keep him informed of what the sibling is up to at any one moment!

The only child is very likely to be pleasant company to most other people, whether in intimate or in casual situations. They are, as Adler says, often very "sweet and affectionate."[2] In childhood it is sometimes especially important to the only child to be "cute" and "appealing" to please parents, and the only child may carry these winning ways into adulthood. A distinguished woman scientist who is an only child often astonishes and somehow charms other people by lapsing, at unexpected moments, into the use of what has been called a "tiny baby voice."

Other people may also especially enjoy being with only children because they tend to be less competitive in their association with them and to engage less in behavior growing out of jealousy of others. The only child usually has received what he has needed or wanted, especially in the area of "things" and so he does not need to be envious of other people. He can easily express appreciation of the achievements or possessions of other people; the person who feels envious cannot easily do this.

The only child enjoys being accepted by other people and especially being drawn in as a part of groups. If he does not feel that he is being accepted as one of a group, he is very likely to experience a resurgence of that childhood feeling of being "left out" of plans and activities by the parents. He has been found, in many studies of the need for affiliation with others, to wish to be with others, especially in situations where a problem is to be solved or anxiety to be overcome.[3]

However, on a day-to-day basis the adult only child has a great need for occasional and sometimes frequent periods of solitude. Usually he had occasion in childhood to spend a great deal of time by himself and he learned to enjoy his own company at times. He often evidences a special antipathy for much noise in his environment, perhaps because his household in childhood was usually noisy only when he made the noise. Only child Mary Astor thus tells of her need for "Just me . . . and blessed quiet."[8]

Since he spent much time in childhood in solitary play and often engaged in elaborate fantasy, the only child tends to enjoy having the time and opportunity in adulthood for quiet thinking.

One of the circumstances that tend to plague the adulthood of the only child is a tendency to be preoccupied with physical conditions and often to treat them with far more seriousness than they might actually deserve. Only children frequently complain of stomach upsets, constipation or diarrhea, feeling "weak" or just "not well"; conditions which are uncomfortable but are rarely diagnosed by medical people as incapacitating. Yet the only child, and especially the female only child, may allow such disorders to interfere seriously with usual activities.

It is in close relationships with other people that the only child may bring into play uncomfortable needs and wishes that sometimes grow out of his special role as the only child in his family. Perhaps for him, more than for persons raised in other family positions, there may be a strong discrepancy between that which appears to other people and that which goes on inside him. Usually the only child is likely to appear quite "parental" in behavior with other people. He may be quick to think of ways to help other people and be ready with suggestions as to how crises and problems may be met. Having been very close to his parents throughout childhood, he took on their adult ways of coping with the world. Thus he presents to other people, particularly those in relatively casual relationships, a usual image of being independent and capable.

But inside the only child may feel quite different from the way other people see him. Having filled the role for many years of being a child with two adults, he continues to feel as a child. Sometimes this condition is accentuated by parents who attempt to shield their only child from unhappiness or trouble by keeping him uninformed about their own problems. An only child who was so sheltered said, "My parents told me nothing about the world or its problems. I've had to learn it all since I was twenty. I feel insecure about being adult. I haven't yet learned how to assume responsibilities as an adult."

Like the youngest child in any family, the only child does not have younger siblings on whom to test his capacities during childhood. He did not have siblings to stimulate development of competitive skills. He had to compare himself in childhood with his parents and, in relation to them, he had to feel that he was relatively incapable of independent and effective achievement. In adulthood, no matter how capable he becomes or is perceived to be by other people, he is likely to have to contend with that "child within." An energetic businesswoman who was forty years old was surprised to be elected chairman of the board: "I feel," she said, "as though they'll find out that I'm really only a little girl who is trying to fit into an adult world."

He is usually able to hide the "child within" in more casual relationships and in the relatively less intimate ones of professional or business colleagues. It is his close and intimate relationships that tend to follow a pattern very much that of an only child.

In adulthood he may retain an unusually close relationship with his parents. This is almost inevitable as a result of his being the one child of the parents; the parents have no other places to take their time and attention within the close family group. The adult only child is often called upon to give a great deal of care to aged or ill parents. Female only children sometimes give up careers and even the possibility of marriage because of a parent who needs help. Death of a parent or the separation or divorce of parents usually means that the child is placed in care of one parent and an intense mutual dependency may result. The child may feel both dependent upon and responsible for the parent, and the parent may encourage the child to feel such responsibility. Sammy Davis, Jr.,[9] describes the slow transition for him of dependency on his father when he was a child to a position of responsibility for his father, and he tells of the limitations which such a relationship places on a developing male only child.

The depth of the relationship between only child and parents is shown even when there is extreme ambivalence about the parents and perhaps even intense hatred directed toward one or both of them. Despite such feelings, the only child tends to retain a feeling of responsibility for his parents. A female only child, who had experienced tremendous anger toward her parents over a long period of time, without hesitation gave them part of her rather meagre salary when her father was ill and unable to work for a time.

The psychological ties can be strong in other ways. Parents sometimes resent giving up their only child to a spouse of that child. The writer Frank O'Connor found after he separated from his wife that his mother had destroyed every photograph of his wife in his album and had cut her picture out of photographs in which she had been shown with either her husband or her children. When Frank O'Connor was fifty years old, he had occasion to say that he might have to leave Ireland. His mother said without a moment's hesitation, "Of course I'll go with you. I know you must be free."[10] This statement seems to exemplify the mutual dependency in such cases: neither of them considered that "freedom" might include freedom from Mother.

In extreme cases an only child may display such a close relationship with a parent that he seems to have no identity as a separate person, only as the child of the parent. As the outcome of a psychological study of a forty-five year old married woman, the examiner wrote, "The patient's relationship with her mother is a symbiotic one which has never been loosened to any appreciable extent. She feels as though she and her mother are almost one person, as though she has no identity other than that of being the child of her mother."

In the area of friendships the only child is likely at any one time to have one or two friends with whom he spends much time and with whom he is close and intimate. The mother of an adult woman told me that she worried because her only child was so intense about relationships with her intimate friends. "She depends on them so much," the mother said. "What they do is so important to her. I'm afraid she will be terribly hurt by one of them someday." And it is generally true that the only child tends to expect a great deal from friends in the way of support, loyalty, attention, and companionship, and to be bewildered and hurt if the friends do not meet these needs. Frank O'Connor tells how he reacted in adulthood, "Friendship did not make me wiser or happier, for years of lonely day-dreaming had left me emotionally at the age of ten. . . . even the suspicion of a slight left me as frantic as a neurotic school girl."[10]

The adult only child is usually quite adroit at hiding inner dependency on his friends. Yet he must watch his tendency to require too much of relationships either in the way of emotional support or in an area in which an only child often leans heavily on friends: for help and assistance in practical matters. Female only children are especially apt to ask friends to run errands or to help them with entertaining or to fill in in ways that the only child's mother did. Sometimes, then, the friendship is short-lived because the friend feels that too much is being required, though this may not even be consciously recognized as a reason for dissatisfaction with the relationship. Only children must be sure that giving is reciprocal in a relationship, whether it is of things or of time or of affection. An only child, for instance, telephoned a busy friend with three small children and announced that she was eating at friends' homes as often as possible because she "had no money and had to save what she had." The friend sympathized until the only child explained that she had to save money so that she could take a trip around the world the next summer and so she needed help. The only child is inclined to concentrate attention on her own plans and wishes and not to recognize the problems (and the wishes) of other people.

The female only child tends to select friends who are not peers; her friends are usually considerably older or younger than she. She often selects older friends during her own adolescence or early adulthood because she looks to them for guidance and general mothering. Later she may select friends who are younger but closer to fitting her own self-concept, but she is very efficient in selecting even younger friends who have a childhood history of being "parental." Thus her younger friend often proves to be an oldest child who tends to be parental in any relationship. The only child is even likely to select strong "mothers" as servants, and they may accept any degree of insubordination from their helpers if they will simply stay as "parent surrogates." An example of this was found in the autobiography of actress Lita Grey Chaplin who clung to her "dresser" like a dependent and helpless child.[11]

The male only child is not as apt to look for "parenting" by friends because he usually, before marriage, retains a relationship with a mother who will fill that role for him. He often does not seem to be much of a swinger during pre-marriage days, and he tends to marry while he is relatively young, unless his relationship with his mother is extremely close and mutually dependent. Often his first sexual experience is with the woman he marries and often he is known as somewhat of a "woman hater" before that time. In many cases, of course, his disinterest in girls his own age is promoted by his mother. But if he finds a girl in whom he is interested and who seems to offer some of the qualities of loyalty and devotion that he finds in his mother, he is not likely to delay his marriage to her.

The only child often seems to marry with even more idealistic and sometimes unrealistic expectations about what the marital relationship is to be like than the average person does. The only child anticipates much from the partner in the way of support and attention. They may, as Dr. Walter Toman tells us, look for a mother or father in their potential spouse.[12] Mary Astor tells us that she grasped at each new relationship as though it offered every promise of support, protection, and concern.

Since the only child is not at all inclined to be a martyr in any relationship, he may drop quite abruptly a relationship that does not meet his requirements. Thus, though the only child is constantly looking for a deeply warm relationship that will alleviate his inner feelings of loneliness and give him the security he felt with his parents, he may seem to move casually from one marriage to another. Many only children who are wealthy tend to marry frequently, being continuously disappointed as they search for the "right" person. One of the reasons this occurs is that the only child tends to appear parental and considerate and thus attracts to himself or herself persons who themselves want to be protected. The only child then discovers in marriage that he cannot obtain from such a spouse the wished for aid and consideration. Mary Astor found in psychotherapy that she had always looked for someone to take care of her and had always selected the wrong person to do so. Even in marriage it is important to the only child to maintain a self-concept of being more the parent than the child in the relationship. So he frequently finds strange justifications for the "babying" he may require. An only child retorted when her husband said that he did some of the housework because she wouldn't do it, "You must like to do it. People only do what they want to do." The only child often reflects the early experience of having a mother and often a father who would take care of the practical aspects of life for him. Neither the male nor the female only child easily accepts the household responsibilities such as cleaning and cooking. Obviously this does not interfere with the role of the male only child as a "good spouse" as much as it might with the role of the female only child. The wife of the male expects to take care of these things for him. The husband of the female only child may, like the man mentioned earlier, find himself participating a great deal in such household activities. Often the female only child will vacillate between being a most self-consciously efficient "wife and housekeeper" and being a dependent and helpless child who must be protected by her husband. The husband of an only child complained that she sometimes "acts more as though she is a little girl playing house than like a grown-up woman." It is very important that the husband of the only child be patient and kind with her because she is not only usually aware of her limitations in taking on mature responsibilities, but she is easily hurt by criticism.

The female only child often does not like to organize social functions and she may be a reluctant hostess for her husband. Not only does she dislike such obligations, but she usually would prefer to have her husband to herself. In this area, the female only child must be very careful to contribute as needed because her husband may not only enjoy such social occasions, but he is also likely to find them helpful in his business or professional relationships.

Both the male and female only children are likely to want to have their spouses much to themselves. Only children, particularly women, may even be most resentful of the time their husbands must spend away from home in order to earn a living. A woman told me that she "missed" her husband even when he left her side at parties. "It hurts me when he talks and smiles at other people. I don't want to be alone."

The spouse of either the male or female only child is likely to find the only child emphatic about obtaining "things." In childhood the only child has come to expect to receive as much as the parents can afford and also to compare his worth with others on the basis of having more "things." The only child is often described by the spouse as "impractical" about money and the spouse is likely to try to keep expenses down. A male only child will sometimes put a great deal of pressure on his wife to earn money to add to the financial resources of the two. An advantage in marrying an only child might be mentioned here: the resources of the in-laws will be concentrated on their one child's family after he marries.

Two only children, who wanted to marry but did not have enough financial support to buy and furnish the kind of home they wanted, developed a rather unusual but effective plan. They married but kept their marriage secret while, by living at home with parents, each of them accumulated a good "nest egg". They then announced their marriage and saw to it that their parents had all the necessary announcements and receptions and showers so that they could have all the usual "trimmings" in the way of gifts.

In a study of engagements and marriages involving only children,[13] it was found that the rate of broken ties differed before and after marriage and with the sex of the only child. The rate of broken engagements was high, which possibly indicates some difficulty in maintaining relationships as long as there are no legal ties.

For male only children, the same study found a high rate of separation and divorce after marriage. There was a low rate of separation and divorce for female only children. Obviously, female "onlies" must manage not to marry male "onlies" in most cases.

The difference in rate between sexes is provocative for discussion. It is possible that the wives of only children are less likely to put up with the underlying dependency of husbands than are the husbands of only children. A husband of an only child may find the dependency of his only child wife rather flattering and acceptable since it occurs in a woman. The charm that an only child can bring to a marriage may sometimes offset the female only child's unwillingness to take care of the practical aspects of homemaking. It must also be taken into account that men are more likely to adjust to adverse circumstances in a marriage than are women. The female only child may remain in a marriage even though it is uncomfortable for both members for the sake of security for herself and for her children.

A male only child will sometimes continue in a relationship with a spouse who seems to be completely cold and rejecting. Often such wives of only children will seem to be constantly attempting to strain the relationship beyond the breaking point by being as unfaithful or unpleasant as possible. A female only child may complain at length about her spouse, but she will usually cling to the relationship nevertheless. The basic tendency of the only child is to cling to the security which is immediately available. There are, however, two conditions which may easily cause the only child to break away from a relationship with someone of the opposite sex.

One condition is the existence of sufficient money so that security is possible without a spouse. The only child may then react quickly to the frustration of needs for acceptance and understanding and make himself available to search once again for satisfaction of these needs.

The other condition has to do with the loyalty of the other person. Only children require attention and companionship in the relation with a spouse, and hence they cannot tolerate any loss of loyalty which requires them to share the time and company of the spouse with anyone else. The male only child often seems better able to tolerate physical infidelity on the part of his wife than that she participate in activities that will take her away from home so that she is not there when he needs her. Male only children have told me of infidelities of their wives while their husbands were on long-extended business trips or perhaps overseas in military service. They seemed often to be quite tolerant and understanding of the wives' behavior—as long as those wives were present to greet them when they arrived home. The male only child seems often to dread loneliness even more than the female only child does and he tends to avoid separation from his wife—unless there is enough money to pay for other constant company. Female only children do not wish to share their spouse with anyone else, and they will often cling to even the most unsuitable spouse in order to maintain some security in a relationship.

The female only child is often fearful of motherhood but quite possessive of her children when she has them. She is likely to place a high value on her status as a "mother." If her child is a boy, she is likely to consider him to be a very special production and possession. To give to him is to enhance her own status. Hence she has no trouble sharing the good things of the family with him.

The situation may be somewhat different if the only child has a girl child. The female only child may then become intensely competitive with her own child, almost as though she now has the younger sibling that she was spared in her childhood. She may compete with her own daughter for the attention of that one male in the household: her husband. On the other hand, if her child is a son, her husband may find himself somewhat excluded because she is likely to concentrate a great deal of attention on the son.

Even with her enthusiasm for motherhood, the tendency of the only child is often to limit the number of children she has. She may have only one child or, according to Dr. Walter Toman, she may be more content than the female from any other family position to remain childless.[14] There may be various reasons for the contentment of the female only child with one child. A need for solitude and quiet is one of them. Another is that she may find it difficult to adjust to the rambunctious play of children when she has always been the only child in the home.

Male only children are sometimes not particularly interested in having children and may agree to this only to please their wives. He tends as a father to be rather warm and companionable with his children when they are very young but to withdraw from them when they are older and demanding of his time and attention. He may be much warmer with his girl children than with his male children, as though he prefers having no competition as the male with his wife who may also be for him a kind of mother surrogate. In extreme cases he may resent his child or children and feel that they take too much of his wife's attention and time, and perhaps that they are more responsibility than he cares to accept. His "child within" may feel competitive with the real children in the home.

Both the male only child and the female only child are likely to be more comfortable if there are two or more children in the home so that these tendencies toward competition with the children can be avoided. It was said in the last chapter that relationships among the three members of the one-child family are often quite intense. If one of the parents is himself an only child, the competition can reach unhealthy levels.

REFERENCES

1. OBERLANDER, MARK, and JENKIN, NOEL: Birth order and academic achievement. *J Individ Psychol, 23:*103-109, 1967.
2. ADLER, ALFRED: *Problems of Neurosis.* New York, Harper & Row, 1964, p. 111.
3. SCHACHTER, STANLEY: *The Psychology of Affiliation.* Stanford, Stanford U Pr, 1959.
4. *Newsweek:* Is First Best? January 6, 1969, p. 37.
5. LAMARR, HEDY: *Ecstasy and Me.* New York, Fawcett World, 1966. p. 82.
6. ALLEN, FRED: *Much Ado About Me.* New York, Little, 1956.
7. GREEN, C. E.: The effect of birth order and family size on extrasensory perception. *J Soc Psychical Res, 43:*181-191, 1965.
8. ASTOR, MARY: *My Story.* New York, Doubleday, 1959.
9. DAVIS, SAMMY, JR.; BOYAR, JANE, and BOYAR, BURT: *Yes I Can.* New York; Farrar, Straus, and Giroux, 1965.
10. O'CONNOR, FRANK: *An Only Child.* New York, Knopf, 1961.
11. CHAPLIN, LITA GREY, with COOPER, MORTON: *My Life With Chaplin.* New York, Geis, 1966.
12. TOMAN, WALTER: Family constellation as a basic personality determinant, *J Individ Psychol, 15:*199-211, 1959.
13. HALL, EVERETTE: Ordinal position and success in engagement and marriage. *J Individ Psychol, 21:*154-158, 1965.
14. TOMAN, WALTER: *Family Constellation.* New York, Springer, 1961, p. 119.

Chapter IX

THE CHILDHOOD OF THE OLDEST CHILD OR "SOMEONE'S PRIDE AND JOY"

THE only child and the oldest child share many conditions of development because they are both first-born children. They are born to parents who are usually more joyfully anticipatory than they may be when later children are expected. These parents are usually more tense and anxious than they will be with later children because they are uncertain of their ability to care for a child. Their inexperience may cause them to expect more of their first child than they will expect of later children and to be more concerned about any physical or mental deviations which their child seems to make from "normality." Thus first-born children tend to be more emotionally volatile than children raised in other positions and to be more susceptible to quick anger. They may be more strong-willed and stubborn than other children.

The first-born children usually have a closer relationship with the parents than later-born children. The oldest child, like the only child, has the experience of having his parents to himself. He is in a position to use them as a direct model. Even after younger siblings arrive, it is still the parents who are a direct source of identification for him. He himself becomes one of the models for the younger children.

Since the oldest child has the full attention of his parents for a period of time, he tends to develop a feeling of being a rather important individual. His development follows the lines described for the only child in the previous two chapters. His adult personality will be much like that of an only child.

Katharine was nine years old when a brother was born. Three years later a sister arrived. Katharine had already given evidence of considerable musical talent, and her parents did not allow the younger siblings to make any difference in Katharine's schedule of lessons and concerts. In young adulthood Katharine's attitude toward her younger siblings was something like that of a rather distant aunt. She was interested enough to give them considerable advice, but she took no part in their daily activities. She felt and acted as though she were the only child of her parents.

Anne was twenty years old when, to the astonishment and consternation of parents and friends, a baby sister arrived. Anne's mother, overwhelmed by what was to her an unwelcome event because she was in ill health, turned the care of the baby over to Anne who was living at home while attending college. This maneuver did not in any way cause Anne to feel motherly toward the baby. Rather she was highly resentful and soon dropped out of school and took a job so she could be free of the responsibility.

Both Katharine and Anne had been only children too long to be much affected in their concepts of themselves when another sibling arrived.

Usually the first-born child is much younger than either of the two girls just mentioned when the next child is born. As welcome as that next child may be to family and friends, his appearance on the scene makes great changes in the life of the first child. The changes may occur slowly and they may be relatively gentle and benign, but they inevitably occur.

The relationship of the first child to his parents is almost immediately changed. He can no longer expect from them the full attention, affection, interest, and gifts that he formerly received. Surely it is to be expected that the first child should react in some way to this unfavorable development. As we discovered in an earlier chapter, his reactions are likely to be most intense if he is between eighteen months and four and a half or five years of age.

It has been my observation that what occurs first in the reactions of the first child is bewilderment and a feeling of having been abandoned. Jealousy is a later development and seems to appear after the child discovers the full extent of the other child's participation in receiving affection, attention, and gifts from the parents. It might be of some interest to us to follow the reactions of a first child as described by a woman who was five years old when a brother was born.

She said that she became bewildered even before the baby was born. "I remember that when my mother was pregnant, there began to be an undercurrent of secrecy in communications between my mother, my father, and their friends. There was giggling and whispering in which I seemed to have no part and I became uneasy and apprehensive. My parents were rather old-fashioned in their notions, but I am sure that I probably was told that I might anticipate having a brother or sister. If I were told, I apparently tried to ignore the possibility. I don't remember that I thought any such thing might happen. Then came a morning when my father came to awaken me and take me to the lying-in home where my mother had given birth to my brother during the night. This was in a small town and my parents were rather poor so they did not have either a medical doctor nor a hospital for my mother. I was to stay with my mother in this home for a few days. I remember my first sight of that wrinkled little red baby lying there beside my mother. I suddenly felt withdrawn from everyone. All of what was happening was so foreign to my usual experience of close, loving care and attention by my parents. It was as though I had to withdraw into some kind of closed situation of my own in order to think about it and to form some way of coping with this change in my life."

Then came a feeling of having been abandoned. "My father left me there in the care of a strange woman and I played with her children who seemed strange to me. I knew that my mother was in another room in the same house, but I was not with her. With her was that ugly little red thing and I was forbidden even to go to her door and look in at her."

Then came depression. "I felt deserted and everything seemed to grow dark and looked unpleasant. Even when we returned home, Mother was still busy with the baby and had little time for me. I had been a happy child but now I became quiet and reserved."

The parents then changed their reactions to the behavior of the first child. "Before that time my parents had been delighted with my singing and general playfulness. Now I was shushed when I sang. Mother was tired and taken up with the care of the baby, who was rather frail during his first months. Before he was born Mother and I had spent a good part of each day walking or playing together. She was quite young and seemed almost like a playmate most of the time. Now she would tell me to play outdoors and to be quiet."

The second child becomes the recognized source of all the problems and angry feelings begin to be directed toward him. "I remember quietly opening a door and looking into the room where that annoying little intruder was napping. He still seemed like a stranger to me. I remember thinking that he looks as though he's going to die. He wasn't that sick; obviously I was using wishful thinking."

After bewilderment and depression and anger came jealousy and competitiveness. "The next Christmas I remember watching my parents with astonishment as they tried to persuade the infant to sit on a rocking horse. He was frightened even though there was a belt to protect him. I begged my father to let me show him that I would sit on the horse and that I wasn't afraid. He was annoyed with me because it seemed to him, I suppose, that I was interested in a toy that was much too infantile for me. He didn't understand that I was simply trying to obtain his interest, attention, admiration once again."

The anger was directed toward the parents who had seemingly withdrawn their interest and support, and the anger was partially expressed through rebellion against the parents. "I had always been a good and obedient child, but that summer I frequently disobeyed my parents. My father spanked me and I began to be afraid of him and to dislike him."

Dr. Alfred Adler has detailed for us the ways in which the oldest child tries to regain favour with his parents after the second child is born. He uses all the methods he used previously when he wished to obtain the attention of his parents. He tries being good, but this may be overlooked because the parents are busy with the newcomer. He may then try the unfavorable tactics that previously received attention from parents. He may be antagonistic and disobedient. Attacks on the baby are a frequent and highly successful way of attracting the attention of the parents. (They have the added advantage of annoying the baby.) The oldest child may return to infantile ways of behaving. He may cease in the development of skills of walking or talking. He may soil or wet again, even though he had previously been toilet trained. He may frequently get into dangerous situations or hurt himself. His tension may bring about headaches or stomach trouble and he may complain of being tired and look exhausted.

Dr. Adler tells us that the way the environment reacts will determine the means used by the child to regain attention and his place in the sun. If fighting wins, he is likely to become a fighting child. If fighting does not win, he may become depressed and use subtle means of misfortune to worry his parents and thus gain his desired end. Unfortunately he "hastens his own dethronement by fighting against it with envy, jealously, and truculence, which lowers him in the parental favour."[1]

The extent to which the child will feel rejected and displaced will depend to a considerable extent upon the real capacity of his parents to be loving, understanding, and considerate. If they are such people, patience and tolerance for their older child will be a matter of course. If parents are unable to draw upon such qualities in themselves, their resolute following of the rules, given in child guidance texts for the proper behavior of parents when a new child is born, will help the situation very little. If they are warm and considerate people, they will make sure that their child never has occasion to develop the original bewilderment and feeling of abandonment that lead to envy and anger.

The first child is subjected to many subtle changes other than loss of the attention of his parents after the birth of a younger sibling.

He is soon expected by his parents to assume new duties and responsibilities. He will feel the effects of being, in their eyes, much more grown-up than they previously perceived him to be. In comparison with the small infant, he is likely to seem relatively mature. They may expect much more mature behavior on his part than they formerly expected. If he is not yet toilet trained, they are likely to be less patient about this than they were previously. It may suddenly seem to them very important that he stop as soon as possible adding to the diapers that must be washed. Since they have a smaller infant to look after, they are likely to expect the older child to assume responsibilities for himself that he did not previously have. He may, for instance, be expected to make his own bed and pick up his own room.

His first reaction may be to regress to earlier infantile ways of behaving in order to evade the responsibilities. He is, however, likely to discover very soon that his parents do not approve of this tactic. They may shame him, become angry with him, and punish him for such transgressions as wetting the bed, soiling, attacking the younger sibling, or defying them.

There is another method that the child can use to regain some of their favour and he usually turns to it eventually. He tries to conform to the parents' standards. He tries to cope with the responsibilities. He tries to be like his parents. He already has a well-established habit of imitating their behavior. Heretofore he could be a child who learned to talk and walk like Daddy, but he did not have to take on responsibilities like those of Daddy. Now the parents are saying in essence: "You must be like us and take responsibility for yourself and for other people." He must cope somehow with that new child in the family. The attitude and behavior that offer the best chance of success in pleasing his parents are those which the parents themselves display. So the older child begins a process of being "parental" in relationships with other people.

He becomes parental in the ways the parents are parental. If they are tolerant and patient with their older child, he is likely to adopt that attitude in fulfilling his responsibilities toward other people. If they are dominating and authoritarian, he is likely to develop in that direction.

Because of his particular situation in the family, he is more likely than other children in his family to be the object of the anger and punishment of his parents. They expect him to take on many responsibilities but he is not, of course, yet mature enough to carry them out in the way the parents expect. He may make his bed, but it is not likely to be made in a way that will please his mother. He forgets sometimes that a bed must be made everyday. If his parents are impatient with him and criticize him for inadequacy, he may assume their evaluation of himself and develop strong feelings of inadequacy that may plague him all his life. Or he may fight their demands for a higher level of effective performance than he can deliver and become angry and rebellious in their eyes.

He will strive still to be close to his parents, and he may make many demands for their attention and time by talking a great deal or by constantly asking for help. He may develop an extreme degree of self-assertiveness and become even more authoritative in his attitude than one or both of his parents.

It will be seen that these approaches of the first-born child toward establishing a place for himself are in the general direction of "acting-out" against the environment rather than withdrawing from it. When the behavior of the first-born child brings him to a behavior clinic, it seems usually to be behavior along the lines of such "acting out." At the State University of Iowa, three investigators found that the disorders of first-born children were in the nature of a "lashing out at the world."[2] The delinquent acts of oldest children have been found to be mainly those of such "offenses against the home" as desertion and parental claims that their children were ungovernable.[3]

In line with such findings about the first-born it has been observed that oldest children who become psychotic may be more likely to develop manic-depressive than schizophrenic symptoms.[4] The symptoms of the former disorder are in the nature of behavior directed against the outside world, while the symptoms of schizophrenia involve more of a withdrawal from it.

As more children are added to the family, the oldest child must continue to make some adjustments in his behavior and attitude, but the trauma is never as great for him as it was when that first sibling was born. When still later siblings arrive, the first child has become accustomed (though not resigned) to receiving only a portion of the parents' time and attention. He has usually fully accepted his need to be more "parental" than "childlike" in his behavior in order to please his parents and to cope with the younger siblings.

There may be many advantages for the first-born child in his position of older and oldest. He develops many skills in the direction of responsibility and leadership. Even in childhood he may take great pride in knowing himself to be more capable, more intelligent, stronger than his siblings.

But if the family grows beyond three or four children, the oldest may lose even such advantages. Dr. James H. S. Bossard[5] concluded after a study of families with six or more children that such large families almost invariably required exploitation of one or more of the older children in the family, and the exploitation often interfered with the life plans of these older children. He found that the oldest children were more likely as adults to express dissatisfaction with their childhood roles than were their siblings from other family positions. These oldest children displayed in general a record of adjustment that was less adequate than that of their siblings. On the other hand, many of them claimed that they felt that they had gained from having maturity forced upon them and from having learned habits of responsibility at an early age.

The experiences of the oldest child often make him seem old beyond his years and often more serious than other children. First-born Sigmund Freud wrote to his fiancee that ". . . in my youth I was never young."[6] The oldest daughter of Charlie Chaplin and first-born of his second family is described by a younger brother as having been ". . . born a thousand years old."[7] A neighbor of mine who believes strongly in reincarnation named several children whom she described as "Old Souls who have lived through many lives." All the children she named were the oldest children in their families!

It is important for parents, who sometimes are extremely uncomfortable in the relationship with their oldest child, to understand that much of his behavior is an attempt at adjustment to sibling competition and an appeal for their affection and attention. While he is adjusting to the existence of sibling rivals for the parents, he is slowly assimilating the parents' standards of what is right and wrong, of what should and should not be done. The rebelliousness that he so often exhibits during this process very often obscures the direction of his development and his parents may believe that he is well on his way to "ruin." They are, then, extremely surprised to see their child change slowly from being a rebellious, angry child or adolescent to a responsible and productive individual in later adolescence or adulthood. It is then apparent that all the time he has been incorporating the standards and values of his parents into his own conscience. The strictness of the parents turns into strictness of the child toward himself. He requires of himself conformity, responsibility, and productiveness. We now find the favorable developments described in Chapter IV to become applicable to the oldest child as a first-born child.

REFERENCES

1. ADLER, ALFRED: *Problems of Neurosis.* New York, Harper & Row, 1964, p. 102.
2. CUSHNA, BRUCE; GREENE, MITCHELL; and SNIDER, BILL C. F.: First born and last born children in a child development clinic. *J Individ Psychol, 20:*179-182, 1964, p. 181.
3. ARMSTRONG, C. P.: Delinquency and primogeniture. *Psychological Clinician, 22:*48-52, 1933. Cited in Murphy, Gardner, *et al.: Experimental Social Psychology.* New York, Harper, 1937, p. 348.
4. BERMAN, H. H.: Order of birth in manic-depressive reactions. *Psychiat Quart, 7:*430-435, 1933.
5. BOSSARD, JAMES H. S.: *The Large Family System.* Phil., U of Pa Pr, 1956.
6. FREUD, ERNST L., Ed.: *Letters of Sigmund Freud.* New York, Basic, 1960, p. 202.
7. CHAPLIN, MICHAEL: *I Couldn't Smoke the Grass on My Father's Lawn.* New York, Ballantine, 1966, p. 29.

Chapter X

THE OLDEST CHILD GROWS UP

THE oldest child may be expected to reach adulthood with a well-developed "parent within." He has usually modeled his behavior upon that of his parents and has adopted many of their attitudes as his own. The behavior and attitudes which he is most likely to have copied in their entirety are those that they displayed in directing and disciplining him, their ways of being parental. Thus he is kind and tolerant or stern and disciplining in relating to other people, and particularly to his own dependents, just as his parents were in reacting to him. His feelings about himself and what he expects of himself will depend, too, upon his parents' attitudes and expectations directed toward him.

In the previous chapter concerning the childhood of the oldest child, developmental conditions were described that suggest the genesis of some of the adult characteristics which he may be more likely to display than adults raised in other family positions. He is likely to be easily angered and his disturbances may last for a rather long time. He may tend to be somewhat resentful and envious of the possessions or positions of others, and consequently to be rather competitive. He may take life quite seriously and lack the ability to be spontaneous and relaxed in most situations. Although he may outwardly seem self-confident, particularly because he is often willing to accept responsibility and leadership, he often suffers from feelings that he is actually inadequate. These last feelings seem to come from his childhood tendency to compare himself with his parents' level of competency and from his constant fear that he could not achieve their standards for him.

Although these qualities suggest that he may not be the most comfortable person for himself or others to live with, they do seem consistent with general achievement and it is in this area that we find him excelling. In earlier chapters we have described his academic and occupational accomplishments. First-born children have been found to be verbally more able. They tend, when from families of four or less children, to make higher high school and college grades than later-born siblings; to be represented in larger numbers in college; and to more frequently go on for graduate study. They have been found more likely than later-borns to be pursuing such professional courses as medicine. Evidence suggests that they may be more likely than later-borns to be listed among the eminent.[1]

Information available suggests that the oldest child develops approaches to work and responsibility which are conducive to achievement. He has been found to have a capacity for consistent application of efforts toward a self-selected goal. For instance, he has been found more likely to continue in psychotherapy than later-borns.[2] He has been found more likely than later-borns to volunteer for extra participation in college course-work.[3] Among the possible meanings of such behavior must be conscientiousness and a willingness to apply effort and to work.

Although the characteristics of the oldest child may support achievement, they are not those most likely to help him win popularity contests. They are most likely to be leaders in situations where intimate contact with others is not frequent, such as in large and complex groups. In smaller groups, where members are in close contact, they have been found no more likely than later-borns to be leaders.[4]

The oldest child tends to have some problems in connection with the acceptance of supervision. Out of the old relationship with his parents can come some competition with authority, represented originally by his parents and in his adulthood by his supervisors. He tends to pit his ideas against those of his supervisor. The best "boss" for him is one who will trust him to carry out a job responsibly and who will leave him in charge of it.

It has been observed that oldest children often tend to avoid the conflict about being supervised by entering into occupational choices where they can work independently. In a recent informal count of psychologists and psychiatrists who were in private practice and thus working independently, six out of the eight were oldest children.

When the oldest child himself is the supervisor or employer, he is very likely to demand high standards of performance from those who work for him. If they are not conscientious, he is unlikely to tolerate them for long. One area where the female oldest child often runs into trouble is in her supervision of household help. She tends to be less tolerant than women from other family positions of inadequate or half-hearted work. She wants the same standards of performance to be met by her helper that she sets for herself and thus, as things are today in the realm of domestic help, both she and her employees are likely to make frequent changes. On the other hand, once convinced of the employee's conscientiousness, both the male and female oldest child tend to show their gratitude in concrete ways and they will be most loyal and supportive toward those employees.

It must be remembered that the "parental" role assumed by the oldest child does not necessarily include kindness, tolerance and being a nurturing person. The oldest child tends to identify with the directive and supervisory aspects of the parents' behavior. Thus he demands obedience and achievement from others. Dr. Karl Konig tells us that the respective birth orders of supervisor and employee can make quite a difference. A first-born supervisor may make a later-born most uncomfortable because he is required to adhere to duty without relaxation or indulgence in pleasure.[5]

We have evidence which suggests that the adult role may be somewhat different for the oldest child in a family of four or less children, than for the oldest child of five or more siblings. It is possible that the oldest of the larger number of children tends to identify more fully with the practical aspects of caring for dependents while the oldest child of the smaller family tends to identify with the directive and supervisory aspects of the parents' behavior. Thus their adult adjustments may be somewhat different, as suggested by some of the childhood variations in role described in the last chapter. We can cite in support of this hypothesis an investigation of the birth order of pediatric nurses. It was considered probable that such nurses were more likely to be oldest children than later-born or only children because they might be accustomed to taking a "motherly" role in relationships with children. The investigators found that a pediatric nurse was more likely to be an oldest child, but only when she had been an oldest child in a large family. Apparently a girl who had been the oldest in a family of four or less children was no more likely to want to care for children than girls from other family positions.[6]

The characteristics, attitudes, and approaches that have been described for the oldest child suggest that he might not be the most comfortable person in close relationships; those of friendship, marriage and of parent and child. His seriousness, his adherence to relatively strict standards of behavior and his imposition of these on others, his tendencies to take charge of situations and to tell others what to do may not make him the most popular person in intimate social situations. It was mentioned above that he is more likely to be a leader in large groups than in small ones. Dr. Reginald Smart found that first-born males indicated their interest in group membership by more often being members of social groups than were later-borns. They were, however, no more likely to be leaders in such groups than the later-borns.[7] In such groups personal likeability may be more important than leadership in obtaining votes of peers, and thus oldest children may not be elected despite their interest in belonging.

Rather exhaustive study has been made of the "need for affiliation" with others of the oldest child. Evidence has been accumulated that first-born subjects, whether oldest or only, may choose to be with others in times when there is anxiety which needs to be alleviated because circumstances are threatening.[2] I think we still need to discover whether this may be so because the oldest child is more dependent on others for support, or if it is so because the oldest feels capable of leading others into successful overcoming of threat.

Dr. Stanley Schachter of Columbia University has been responsible for many of the studies of the "affiliation" needs of the oldest child. In a study along somewhat different lines,[3] he found that first-borns (both "onlies" and oldest) tended to select, as preferred contacts among other members of their fraternities and sororities, persons who were "socially desirable" on the basis of popularity, wealth, social class, etc. On the other hand, they themselves were found to be considerably less popular than later-borns. This discrepancy between the relationships they wish to have and those they actually may have suggests considerable discomfort in inter-personal relationships for the oldest and "onlies." (It is studies such as the one just cited that suggest the great need for separate consideration of oldest and only children as subjects. In the chapter about only children we found evidence that they are often popular choices and often so because they tend to come from families of higher social and financial status.)

Oldest children may be somewhat more sensitive in relationships with other people than later-born and only children. We mentioned earlier the findings of a study in England where oldest children displayed signs of ability for extra-sensory perception though others did not.[9] Although the study did not support existence of ESP as a special ability, it did suggest that oldest children might be more sensitive to small cues concerning interpersonal reactivity than persons from other family positions might be.

We also have some evidence that suggests that first-borns may be less likely to harm physically other people than are later-borns when involved in anti-social acts.[10] First-born convicts have been found less likely to have committed crimes against persons than convicts from other sibling positions.[11]

In their day-to-day behavior oldest children tend to evidence some reluctance to involve themselves in close, intimate relationships with other people. They do not seem, whether male or female, to be as likely to have a few very close friends as to have a number of acquaintances. Often, if there is a close, intimate friend, that friend will be found to be an only child or a youngest child who is able to accept the parental attitude of the oldest child, because along with it goes a good deal of care and service. The oldest child will, in turn, experience the gratification of feeling more competent and adequate than the other person.

Since Dr. Stanley Schachter had found evidence that oldest children might be more dependent on others than later-borns, and that they might have learned that being with others in an anxiety-provoking situation is anxiety-reducing, Dr. Peter H. Murdoch of the University of North Carolina hypothesized that they would then tend to marry earlier than later-borns. He found that his data supported the finding for male oldest children, but that there seemed to be no significant relationship between birth order and marriage age for female oldest children. However, it occurred to Dr. Murdoch that female oldest children might not have as much choice in the matter as male oldest do. It is, after all, the males who do the proposing. He then followed up with a study of women's preference as to "mean-best-marriage" age and found that first-born females did express a preference for lower marriage ages than did later-born females.[12]

Thus it seemed that, while females had less choice in the matter than males did, they would have liked to marry earlier as did their male counterparts.

There are other suggestions that female oldest children may have a more difficult time with marital relationships than does the male oldest child. Not only does she tend to be married later than he and later than she wishes to be, but the divorce rate has been found to be relatively high for her while it has been found relatively low for the male oldest child.[13]

There are many reasons that arise out of the birth order of the oldest child that give us a basis for explaining the relative discomfort of the female oldest child in marriage and the relative comfort of the male oldest child.

We may return a few paragraphs to Dr. Murdoch's recognition of a basic difference between the sexes: the man proposes. Although the woman may have a very definite idea from the beginning of their association that she wants this man, she usually has to wait until he gets around to proposing before marriage actually takes place. Thus she is dependent to a considerable extent on who wants her as a wife. Dr. Walter Toman[14] found that oldest brothers tended to choose youngest sisters to be their wives. Oldest sisters, more often than chance, were chosen as wives by youngest brothers.

Younger or youngest brothers tend to be relatively relaxed and passive in their relationships. They often are not driven by a need for domination and achievement as are oldest brothers and oldest sisters. Thus oldest sisters may try to dominate their seemingly less determined spouses and make those spouses so uncomfortable that the marriage does not last. Or oldest sister may actually accept a spouse who really is less adequate than she and who becomes dependent on her. She may do this out of unconscious needs to continue her childhood role of being the stronger, more capable one. Or the need of the relatively inadequate male may, for a time, be overshadowed by his love and admiration of her.

The greatest danger for the female oldest child is that she might marry someone who is severely inadequate. Sometimes she seems so much to enjoy "mothering" a man that she does not examine the reason for his accepting dependency. She may overlook such serious indications of pathological dependency as a tendency toward alcoholism or a history of non-employment or shifting employment. Sometimes she is so sure that she can handle things until he "gets on his feet" that she fails to perceive that his history suggests that he never will. It is extremely important that oldest sister should examine carefully her relationship with a man she wishes to marry so that she can be sure she is marrying one who wants her as "wife" and not as "big sister." Since she tends to place a high value on achievement, she will easily lose respect for a man who does not achieve.

On the positive side, an oldest sister is often a great help to her husband because she tends to take a great deal of responsibility for their children, which leaves him free to use his attention and energy in furthering his career and their financial status. She often, too, contributes a great deal to his career by organizing and directing his social life and thus aids him in relationships with colleagues.

An interesting and sometimes rather painful tug-of-war occurs between a husband and wife when both are older or oldest children. Such a combination often makes for a great deal of worldly achievement on the part of the couple, but they often find it difficult to satisfy each other's emotional needs. The wife will attempt sometimes to prove that she can really dominate her husband and she may, for a long time, have a conscious or unconscious belief that she is more adequate than he. The husband will feel his wife's attempts to dominate him and may even feel, at an unconscious level, that she is causing him to be less confident of himself as a male. This, of course, challenges both his happiness and the endurance of the marriage.

The male oldest child is likely to be a responsible husband for a woman in almost any sibling position. It is expected that the male should take a leading position in marriage and most women will take satisfaction in having their husbands do so. Although the wife of the male oldest child may be somewhat uncomfortable because he tends to be strict in enforcing rules both for her and for their children, she is relatively able to accept other tendencies to be authoritative and dominating, possibly because he is also willing to accept a great deal of responsibility.

As we have said, the male oldest child tends to select as wives, women who are younger or youngest sisters and with whom he can have a comfortable feeling of relative adequacy and aggressiveness. Even when he is married to an oldest child, he is very likely to feel more comfortable and less competitive than she. In his childhood position as oldest son he became accustomed to maternal control of the practical aspects of his everyday life and as long as his wife does not compete with his more masculine pursuits of money and career status, he is likely to let her dominate the rest of his life.

The oldest child may find it difficult to be as tolerant, gentle, relaxed, and warm toward his children as the ideal parental relationship might require. He is likely to be somewhat authoritarian and dominating and the extent to which he is sternly disciplining will usually depend upon the way he himself was raised by his parents. Both male and female oldests are likely to be relatively exacting in their standards for their children.

A particular problem arises for the first child of any older or oldest child. Often this second generation oldest child becomes excessively rebellious, tense, and angry. The possibility that this might occur increases when the first child is a third or fourth generation first child. He receives the full impact of rigid consciences and disciplinary attitudes. In such cases it is very important for parents to develop tolerance and gentleness in their relations with their child.

REFERENCES

1. Altus, William D.: Birth order and its sequelae. *Science, 151:*44-49, 1965.
2. Schachter, Stanley: *The Psychology of Affiliation.* Stanford, Stanford U Pr, 1959.

3. Suedfeld, Peter: Birth order of volunteers for sensory deprivation. *J Abnor Soc Psychol, 68*:195-196, 1964.
4. Smith, Ewart E., and Goodchilds, Jacqueline D.: Some personality and behavioral factors related to birth order. *J Appl Psychol, 47*:300-303, 1963.
5. Konig, Karl: *Brothers and Sisters.* Blauvelt, St. George Books, 1963.
6. Fischer, Ann: The importance of sibling position in the choice of a career in pediatric nursing. *J Health Hum Behav, 3*:283-288, 1962.
7. Smart, Reginald G.: Social-group membership, leadership, and birth order. *J Soc Psychol, 67*:221-225, 1965.
8. Schacter, Stanley: Birth order and sociometric choice. *J Abnor Soc Psychol, 68*:453-456, 1964.
9. Green, C. E.: The effect of birth order and family size on extrasensory perception. *J Soc. Psychical Res, 43*:181-191, 1965.
10. Shield, J. A., and Grigg, A. E.: Extreme ordinal position and criminal behavior. *J Crim Law Criminol, 35*:169-173, 1944.
11. Luthra, B. R.: A study of some convicts in the Central Prison, Naini. *Shiksha, 9*:117-129, 1957. Abstract in *Psychol Abst,* 1959, No. 4302.
12. Murdoch, Peter H.: Birth order and age at marriage. *Brit J Soc Clin Psychol, 5*:24-29, 1966.
13. Hall, Everette: Ordinal position and success in engagement and marriage. *J Individ Psychol, 21*:154-158, 1965.
14. Toman, Walter: Choices of marriage partners by men coming from monosexual sibling configurations. *Brit J Med Psychol, 37*:43-46, 1964.

Chapter XI

THE CHILDHOOD OF THE MIDDLE CHILD
OR "IS HE LOST?"

TRADITION tells us that the middle child usually is in an unfortunate position in his family and that he grows up feeling he has little identity or status within that family. He has been described as threatened by severe feelings of insecurity and inadequacy because he lacks recognition within his family. It has been said that he is in danger of not receiving enough affection, and that he suffers from lack of attention.

Let us see if the information we have been able to find supports these statements about the middle child.

Certainly the middle child has been neglected by scientific investigations into the effects of family ordinal position. He has been included as a subject in studies of "later-born" children, but the qualities of his "middleness" have rarely been studied. He does not offer himself, of course, as a definitive subject as does the only, oldest or youngest child. His position may vary widely from family to family. He may be the middle child of three children or he may be only one of the middle children in larger families. He may be the older of two middle children or the oldest of many middle children. He may be the younger of two middle children or the youngest of many middle children. Although he has the choice of being only one sex or the other, he may have any combination or complexity of brothers or sisters.

As we try to understand a middle child, we must review the circumstances that seem to be of importance for the development of any child born after the first child in the family. The presence of a predecessor means that the parents are more experienced and hence more comfortable in their role as parents than they were with their first child. Consequent upon the greater relaxation of the parents, later children are likely to be more relaxed and less driven, than the first child. Their parental identifications are likely to be less severe and disciplining, both of themselves and others, than those of the first child. The pressures of parents on their second or later children are likely to be relatively well adapted to the mental, emotional, and physical immaturity of the child. With each child that arrives in the family, there seems to be a greater degree of tolerance and relaxation on the part of the parents.

For a period of time the middle child is the younger or youngest child in his family. Since he is not the only child, he is not likely to receive the intense and concentrated care and attention that the first child receives. For awhile he is the "baby" of the family and has the experience of having three or more older and stronger people available to give him aid when he needs it. As a result of all these circumstances, he is likely to develop a recognition that no unusual demands will be put on him and that he can expect help from others when he needs help.

The middle child is never an only child, unless unusual circumstances require that he be taken out of his natural family surroundings. Under customary circumstances he must from the beginning of his existence share the good things of the family with another child or with other children. He does not tend to develop a feeling of omnipotence as often does the first child of a family. He never feels that he owns the parents and his relationship with them is usually not as close and intense as that of the only or oldest or even the youngest child in the family. It is not that the parents do not love him as much; it is just that everyday contact with them is usually divided with other siblings.

He is, of course, the younger or youngest for awhile and has the experience of being supplanted by a new baby. But because he never had the parents to himself, he does not seem to suffer as much shock from dislocation as the "baby" as did the first child when the next child was born. He is likely to feel some jealousy and resentment, especially if he is between eighteen months and four or five years of age, but these reactions are usually less severe than those of the first child.

When a younger sibling is born, the middle child does not lose the position of being younger than another child in the family; he gains the advantage of being older than one or more. Not only does he have to accept some supervision and domination by one or more peers; he has an opportunity to learn how to supervise and direct peers.

These, then, are some of the conditions that suggest that the middle child can be in an advantageous position as compared with other children in the family. His birth order does not compel development of stern authoritarianism and overly serious purpose as does that of the oldest child. He does not have to undergo domination by all other members of the family as does the youngest child.

The characteristics which the middle child may develop as a result of being in his place in the family, and his general comfort with his position seem to depend on the following four conditions: (1) the sex of the middle child, (2) the sex of siblings, (3) the number of children in the family, and (4) where the middle child stands within the group of middle children in his family.

Let us look first at the circumstances surrounding the middle child of only three children. This child was, of course, the second child of his parents. Therefore he will develop at the beginning of his life along the same lines as any second child and he will have the same behavioral tendencies. If we refer back to the chapter on the Two-Child Family, we will find that the sex of the first child and the sex of the second child are important factors in determining how the second child reacts to his position. If the first child is a girl, the second child of either sex may have some difficulty in adjusting to his sibling role. If the first child is a boy, the second child of either sex may have a relatively comfortable adjustment to the role.

In a three-child family, a middle child may be one of three boys or three girls. He or she may be the only boy or girl among the children. Or the middle child may be one of two children of the same sex, and the sibling of the same sex may be older or younger. So we see what complications and permutations we get into when we try to talk even about the simplest situation of the middle child—that of being the middle of only three children. Is it any wonder that scientific investigators have tended to avoid using the middle child as a subject!

On the basis of the information I have been able to obtain, I am going to make the categorical statement that the middle child seems to be in the most precarious situation for his comfort and development, if he is the middle one of only three children, and that the difficulty of the position is increased for the middle child if all three children are female.

Parents usually make a conscious effort to distribute their affection and attention equally among all of their children, but Dr. M. H. Krout[1] thought he might find that they tend to prefer the children holding certain positions in the family over those in other situations without conscious recognition of this. If this were true, it would be one of the circumstances that would cause differences among children from the various ordinal positions in families. Dr. Krout found that the "filial" value of an individual to his parents is in inverse proportion to the number of children of the same sex in the family. In other words, the more children of the same sex in the family, the less likely the parents were to prefer one of them. Dr. Krout also concluded that parents least prefer a female child who is either preceded by another female or followed by another female. These conditions certainly pin-point the middle child of three females as the one most likely to be rejected by the parents. Such a finding supports our observation that the middle girl of three female children will often assume interests quite different from those of her sisters, possibly as a way of achieving status. Sometimes she has emphasized intellectual activities and career rather than taking on the housewifely and motherly interests of her older and younger sisters. A number of women have told me of middle sisters who remained single while their sisters married and had families, and usually this is described as a condition very much to be pitied and avoided. But I should like to offer some consolation to middle sisters in such a position by telling them about the unmarried middle sister who had a successful career and who commented to me the day before she left for a world's tour on a luxury liner: "At last I can see how lucky I was to escape all that business of doing dishes, washing diapers, and trying to make ends meet!"

The middle child of three boys often shows, by relative lack of aggressiveness and striving for achievement, that he was originally a younger brother. In terms of the values of our society, the middle brother may be the least achieving among the siblings, but he may be more comfortable and contented with his lot. Dr. William D. Altus found in a study of illiterate soldiers that the middle child from a family of three was most likely to exhibit good adjustment.[2] We might assume that good adjustment in this situation might require comfortable emotional stance rather than scholarship or relatively high intelligence.

A middle child who is "the first of his sex" in the family is likely to be in a better position than the child who is second of his sex. Thus a girl who follows a boy or a boy who follows a girl is likely to be specially cherished by the parents and to move toward strong identification with the parent of the same sex.

But the sex of the child who follows that second child is also important to the second child. If the middle child is a boy and his older and younger siblings are girls, it is extremely important that his relationship with his father be close and warm. He needs to be with his father a great deal so that he has full opportunity to identify with him. If the boy's relationship with his father is not close, if his father does not give him affection, attention, and time, the boy is subjected to an undue amount of contact with only females. He is very likely then to establish a somewhat weak identification with male aspects of development. From whom can he learn how to be a male? The parents of one small boy in such a family position became distressed when they observed that he was becoming very interested in playing dolls with his sisters and in using their clothes. His father was a highly successful lawyer who had great ambitions for his only son but took little interest in his activities because they were "childish" and "boring." He also said that he was far too busy with important matters to spend time with a child; he would be a companion to his child when he was older. When his attention was directed to the problems his attitude made for his son, he was able to make room in his life for the boy and the boy's interest in female activities soon waned.

A middle child who is the first daughter in the family is likely to be rather comfortable with her role. Even if she is the only girl among the three children, she is unlikely to move toward a masculine identification. As the only girl in the family she is likely to have a special position of close contact with her mother and thus much opportunity to identify with her.

In the four-child family there are two middle children. The

older of these two children may feel quite competitive with the oldest child, particularly if both of the first children are of the same sex. When a fourth child is born into the family, the second child becomes an "older" child and seems to move closer to identification with one or other of the parents. Apparently some loss of status may be felt even in being displaced as *the* middle child. A woman who was the older of two middle girls remembered how she felt when the fourth child was born. She said, "I felt so unhappy because I then wasn't even the middle child. I felt that I was just nothing!" Out of such feelings of loss of status may arise attempts to obtain recognition, and the child is likely to follow the path of the oldest and decide that being as much as possible like the three authorities in the family, the two parents and the older sibling, is the way to do it.

The second of two girls often competes with her older sister as "mother" of the two younger children, and often she has a real advantage in being second rather than first. Like most second children, she tends to be less harsh and restrictive than oldest sister and is likely to end up being the preferred one of the family. In adulthood she sometimes "mothers" all the members of her family, including her parents.

The younger of the two middle children in the four-child family tends to identify as "one of the younger children" and to develop much like a youngest child.

As we describe the four-child family, the four girls in *Little Women*, by Louisa May Alcott,[3] might be cited as typical of such a family. The role described for each of the four daughters so exactly fits our research findings that it seems possible that the great popularity of the book through several generations might be related to the accuracy with which it reflects the situation to be expected in real-life families.* First is oldest sister, Meg, who is a kind and concerned mother-substitute for the young girls. Next is Jo, playful and dreamy but giving Meg help in mothering the younger girls. Gentle and delicate Beth is third, seeming to support Dr. Karl Konig's[4] belief that the third child in a family is often a saint or a martyr. Last and fourth is pretty Amy who captures

* Only after this was written did I discover that Miss Alcott based the book on her family.

the heart of the wealthy boy-next-door, showing once again that the youngest child may not only expect indulgence from the world but often receives it!

If the older of the two middle children is a first son, he may not only identify strongly with his father, but he may also be required to assume practical responsibilities that a second girl would not be asked to assume. In adulthood, even though he has an older sister, he may have to take over as "head of the household" for his mother. Such a middle child responded to a comment about the extent of the business responsibilities he had taken for his entire family: "Of course. I'm the oldest son."

As the family size increases, changes occur in the degree of comfortable adjustment to be expected in each of the ordinal sibling positions. In the chapter on "The Childhood of the Oldest Child" we described the strong possibility that the first child in a large family would suffer both in childhood and in adulthood from exploitation of his ability to help with the younger children. As the family grows larger, the second child may also be asked to take over responsibilities for the younger children. Dr. James H. S. Bossard[5] found, in his study of six or more children, that the poorest record of adult adjustment was for the first-born child and that the next poorest record was for the second oldest child, the first of the middle children.

In Dr. Bossard's study, inbetween children were more often satisfied with their birth positions than were first-born children, but the most satisfactory positions according to those who held them were those of being either fourth or fifth child in these large families. Not one of the holders of these positions expressed dissatisfaction with them and their siblings seemed more envious of them than of the holders of other family positions. The best adult record of adjustment was made by the holders of fourth place in these families and they had relatively better records for marital happiness than their siblings.

If the reader is the parent of a large family or was a member of such a family in his childhood, he will find an interest in *The Large Family System: An Original Study in the Sociology of Family Behavior* by Dr. James H. S. Bossard.[5] An important trend, described by Dr. Bossard, is the development of identity by each child through the assumption of a role which is distinctly different from that of any other child in the family and is largely assigned that child by the other members of the family. The process of assumption of role is said, by Dr. Bossard, to be as follows in the large family: The first child usually becomes the responsible one. The second child attempts to gain recognition and status through personal charm and he makes himself the agreeable one in the family. The next children, the third, fourth, fifth, tend to emphasize social interests outside the family or they become the studious members. The last child in the family may be the "spoiled one" or, on the other hand, he may receive the final pressure of the parents toward high achievement.

The fourth and fifth children, whose places seem to result in most satisfactory adjustment, tend to take roles, which require them to direct their interests outside themselves and outside their families. This would form a basis for the development of skill in relating to others which would, in turn, make for better personal and marital adjustment.

It is uncommon to find a study which points to any degree of maladjustment among children from middle family positions. Usually they are found less likely to evidence disturbed behavior than the only, oldest, or youngest children. Various studies have found them less likely than the others to be on the roles of disturbed kindergarten children,[6] maladjusted adolescents,[7] and convicts.[8]

As research findings accumulate on the effects of being raised in intermediate sibling positions, it seems likely that the favorable position of all but the middle child of three will be established. The intermediate child is forced to be relatively independent and to assume responsibility for himself. He has an opportunity to learn ways of leading and directing others without being forced to assume complete responsibility until he is ready to do so. It may be most important of all that his position requires him to be adjustable and flexible in meeting the various requirements of the older and younger persons in his family.

REFERENCES

1. Krout, M. H.: Typical behavior patterns in twenty-six ordinal positions. *J Genet Psychol, 55*:3-30, 1939.

2. ALTUS, WILLIAM DAVID: Birth order, intelligence, and adjustment. *Psychol Rep, 5:*502, 1959.

3. ALCOTT, LOUISA MAY: *Little Women.* New York, Dutton, 1948.

4. KONIG, KARL: *Brothers and Sisters.* Blauvelt, St. George Books, 1963.

5. BOSSARD, JAMES H. S.: *The Large Family System.* Phil., U of Pa Pr, 1956.

6. STARK, SIEGFRIED: Symptom und geschwister-position in spiegal einer verhaltungsboobachtung (Symptom and sibling constellation in the mirror of an observation of behavior). *Prax. Kinderpsychol. Kinderpsychiat., 11:*177-187, 1962. Abstract in *Psychol Abst,* 1963, No. 6497.

7. PRAKASH, JAI, and SRIVASTAVA, PRAMOD K.: The effect of family size, economic conditions, and order of birth on adolescent adjustment. *Manas, 10:*83-88, 1963.

8. SHIELD, J. A., and GRIGG, A. E.: Extreme ordinal position and criminal behavior. *J. Crim Law Criminol, 35:*169-173, 1944.

Chapter XII

THE MIDDLE CHILD IN ADULTHOOD
OR "A PLEASANT SURPRISE"

THE findings discussed in the last chapter suggest that the middle child may be expected to have a more satisfactory adult adjustment along ordinary lines than the individual coming from any other family position.

The general consensus of previous studies has been that the middle child is less likely than first-born or youngest children to attain eminent status. Since the eminent persons cited in these studies usually attained their positions through unusual scholarship, it seems possible that the conclusions might be different if a wider interpretation were made of "eminence." Many of the most successful politicians in the United States—our national Presidents —have been middle children. Is it possible that the position of middle child may add to the learned skills of taking responsibility for others and adjusting to the needs of others, such abilities as adjustable Machiavellian ways and the imposition of personal charm which make eminence along such lines as politics particularly feasible?

The middle child, especially the one who is among the older children in the family seems to be ambitious and competitive in many ways, but at the same time to be forced to learn ways of competing that are indirect. He learns early to arbitrate as he relates to other people. The means the middle child uses may vary from complicated kinds of Machiavellianism to what might be termed simply sneakiness. In fact, middle children will often be heard to use the word "sneaky" to refer to other people. The approach emphasized by them is often that of being tactful and diplomatic. It seems possible that the middle child may make his way in occupations where personal charm, ability to arbitrate, and the ability to manipulate rather than to take direct action involving others, are important characteristics. Politics, statesmanship, salesmanship are perhaps the kinds of occupations in which middle children might be found to attain superior status.

The female middle child is likely to be content to be directed by others, unless she was the second child in a large family. She is very likely to obtain more satisfaction through enjoyment of the accomplishments of her husband than through exercise of her own aggressiveness and competitiveness. The motivation which may be more important in directing her adult role could be that of becoming a better "mother" than any of her older sisters are.

Some studies of the effects of birth order suggest that college students who were intermediate children tend to feel less dominant than oldest children.[1] However, they are likely to be more patient, stable, and emotionally controlled than those oldest children. (They do not seem to need to hold a certain role in relation to other people in order to feel status or recognition.) The oldest child, for instance, often requires the role of "parent" even in adulthood to feel that he is achieving; the youngest child often wishes to be in a position of child with others; while the only child vacillates between one role and another but often requires the center of the stage. The intermediate child has developed considerable balance between the opposing forces. Thus his behavior in adulthood is not as likely to be dependent on the relationship between him and specific qualities of the other person, as it is for siblings from other positions. At the University of Nottingham in England, J. P. Lees followed-up on the achievement of adult miners who had been given an opportunity to "better their lots" by special education.[2] The oldest children seemed to achieve only if their siblings had already done so, but the behavior of the middle children was not related to that of their siblings. They had their independent wishes for improvement of their "lots in life."

In social groups, the middle child is usually gregarious and friendly. They are used to being in the midst of a number of people and to having little privacy; hence they usually enjoy having much going on around them. They usually learned at an early age that they could not hold the center of the stage for any length of time and they are usually more willing to share it than the child from any other family position.

The middle child seems to be less rigid in his choice of friends than persons from other sibling positions. Dr. Walter Toman studied friendships of boys in an European school. He found that only children tended to prefer only children and older brothers of brothers. Older brothers preferred younger brothers as friends and vice versa. The middle children were the least particular about their friendship choices and more often were the members of trios or quartets of friends.[3] An example of a person who was a middle child and who was able to get along with many different kinds of people at many different social and economic levels was Bernard Baruch, Wall Street billionaire and adviser to Presidents. Second son in a family of four boys, he watched closely the reaction of his Wall Street acquaintances and learned from them ways to manipulate situations so that he became one of the wizards of the stock market. He became, as adviser to several Presidents of the United States, typically not the leader but the "power behind the throne."[4]

The middle child is likely to get along well with members of the opposite sex of any age. Usually middle children will have been raised with siblings of the opposite sex, and they are experienced in considering and meeting the needs of persons both older and younger than themselves.

As we learned in the last chapter, the middle child is likely to be a good matrimonial risk and among them the child from fourth place has an unusually good record. Adjustable and sharing, they tend to adapt their lives so that they can support and meet the needs of their spouses. This seems to be particularly true of the woman who was raised as a middle child.

The middle child is likely to obtain great satisfaction through the parental experience. The female middle child is likely to obtain particular satisfaction, even more so than is usual with a woman from any sibling position, in becoming a mother. In childhood she had to compete with both her mother and any older sisters in "mothering" the younger children. Thus it is extremely satisfying to her to become a mother in her own right.

Middle children of both sexes tend to be relatively more comfortable as parents than are only, oldest, or youngest children. They are likely to be less possessive and competitive with their children than only children are; less dominating and controlling than the oldest; and less impatient than the youngest child.

REFERENCES

1. EISENBERG, P.: Factors relating to feelings of dominance. (Paper delivered at Annual Meeting, Eastern Branch of American Psychological Association), 1937. Cited in Murphy, Gardner, *et al.*: *Experimental Social Psychology.* New York, Harper, 1937.
2. LEES, J. P.: The social mobility of a group of oldest-born and intermediate adult males. *Brit J Psychol, 43:*210-221, 1952.
3. TOMAN, WALTER: Family constellation as a basic personality determinant. *J Individ Psychol, 15:*199-211, 1959.
4. BARUCH, BERNARD M.: *Baruch: My Own Story.* New York, Pocket Books, 1957.

Chapter XIII

THE CHILDHOOD OF THE YOUNGEST CHILD OR "IS HE A SPOILED BRAT?"

T HE youngest child shares with the only child the condition of being a frequent target of popular generalizations. It is said that he is indulged and otherwise "babied" by his parents and that he very often ends up "spoiled."

Despite the fact that his position as the last-born is relatively easy to differentiate from other family positions, he is not often isolated as a subject of study as is the first-born of the family.

An obvious condition of his ordinal position is that he is born to parents who are relatively well experienced in the business of raising children. It is likely that his parents will care for him with more assurance and relaxation than they felt while caring for the first children in the family. They also tend to discipline him less strenuously than they do earlier children in the family. Although Father tends to assume discipline of all other boys in the family, the youngest child, whether boy or girl, is likely to remain the disciplinary responsibility of the mother.[1] He usually receives less physical punishment than the older children in the family. He seems less often than older siblings to be subject to excessive demands from his parents for achievement[2] and that he assume a great deal of responsibility.

For these reasons and possibly others, youngest children have been found in many cases to be more spontaneous, original and creative than children from earlier ordinal positions.

A second condition to which the youngest child is subject is the presence of at least four other persons in the family when he puts in an appearance. These are, of course, his parents and his siblings, and they are older, stronger, and wiser than he. Their presence is advantageous in some ways. They usually give him a great deal of attention, care, and assistance. They stimulate him intellectually both by their examples of accomplishments and by presenting him with so much advanced information. Their presence may also offer some disadvantages. They may encourage the youngest to remain immature and infantile. The older siblings may make him into a kind of "doll" to be played with and cared for but not to be taken seriously. This is one way they may deny his importance in the eyes of their parents and establish their own relative superiority.

His position may also offer him some reasons to feel somewhat inadequate and inferior. His parents may be less interested in his actual accomplishments than they were in the accomplishments of earlier children in the family. It is very likely that the oldest child will receive more acclamation from the parents when he brings home the footstool he made in woodshop than the youngest will when he brings home his! It may be for such a reason that youngest children often seem to lack motivation to achieve along occupational lines.

There is perhaps a more important reason the youngest child may remain relatively passive and submissive. Although no later child is born to displace him and he therefore does not seem to suffer such strong feelings of jealousy as do early born siblings, he does not have an opportunity to sharpen skills of competition and leadership on a younger sibling. He never has the satisfaction of feeling totally more capable than another child in his family. He experiences domination by others and as a result of it may often feel relatively less adequate than they. Like the only child he does not have the opportunity to learn how to dominate others.

The youngest child usually shows a wish to keep up with the older children. My sister used to call her youngest child "Putt-Putt" because she was so often seen trying to catch up with the older children, fat legs plodding, like a small puffing engine trying to keep up with two large locomotives.

A frequent adjustment of the youngest is to find strength in his very weakness. He may not seem motivated to develop constantly a new level of maturity in basic skills, as though it is important to him to remain dependent and with no challenge to compete with others. His resolution of the fear to compete along these lines often shows itself in the retention of immature forms of speech.

Sometimes they will not learn ways of taking care of themselves, such as dressing themselves, because that would mean less attention from Mother. One youngest child did not learn to tie his shoelaces until he was nine years of age because his father did it for him every morning.

The youngest child may be subject to more dilemma when he strives to obtain status than is the child in any other position. Like most other human beings, he wishes to be seen as important and capable. But there are at least four other people in his family on whose toes he might tread if he tries to compete with them. Psychology professor, scholar, and writer Edward G. Boring was the youngest child and only boy in his family. He tells us in his autobiography that he continuously wished for power and for love and that he expended a great deal of effort trying to resolve the contradiction of the two needs.[3] It is extremely important to the youngest child that he retain the love of the other members of his family, but at the same time he wants to develop strength and ability that is acknowledged. Sometimes in childhood he adopts a stance which loses him no love, at least of the parents, and still gives him the powerful feeling of overcoming the siblings. He learns that his screams will quickly bring him the support and attention of Mother and will, on the other hand, bring discipline by Mother to those older siblings. The youngest child, too, may develop a habit of tattling on others as a way of establishing his position as being on the side of the parents and, at the same time, utilizing his strength in competing with the siblings.

Screaming and tattling are special kinds of manipulative skills. They call the attention of authorities to the situation and do not involve direct action by the person himself. As he grows older the youngest child may be more likely to use pleading, whining and complaining to get what he wants rather than temper tantrums or direct, aggressive action. Tears come readily to him when he wants something.

The presence of at least two older siblings means that the youngest child often has a less close relationship with the parents than the older children had during their early childhoods. His parents are relatively less accessible for help and care than they were for the oldest child because three or more children now share their time and energy. Older siblings will often exact considerable penalty when they aid him, by establishing the fact that they thereby show how much more adequate they are. Thus the youngest tends to develop indirect ways of obtaining what he wishes. If this procedure is not successful, he may turn to "giving in" to the demands of others and rarely fighting actively for what he wants. If his parents do not respond positively when he screams, tattles, and whines about others, he may eventually withdraw and become rather passive. In his childhood the problems he brings to clinics seem often to be different from those brought by oldest or older children. The youngest child with a serious problem is likely to be withdrawn,[4] while the oldest child is more likely to show aggressive acting out.

The youngest child is more likely than his older siblings to experience the loss of one or both parents. Since his parents are older, they are more subject to physical ills and he may lose them through serious illness, separation or through death. Obviously he will be a youngest child if marital troubles bring about separation or divorce of his parents.

There is a great deal of evidence that the loss of a parent during early years may have a very adverse influence on the emotional development of a child. The fact that the youngest child is more likely than the child in any other position to experience such a loss may be a reason that hospital populations of schizophrenics often are found to have a large proportion of youngest children.[5]

It was said above that the youngest child has a tendency to withdraw from other people when there is tension or threat in the environment. It was therefore hypothesized that youngest children might be more likely to become alcoholics than children from other family positions. Alcohol, it was believed, would permit retreat of the youngest child from other people. And in several studies the hypothesis was confirmed; it did seem that youngest children were more likely to be alcoholics than their older siblings.[6] But in a follow-up study youngest children were found to be in relatively greater numbers only among alcoholic patients who had been deprived of one or both parents. When alcoholic patients had been raised by both parents, no significant birth order was found.[7] It seems, then, that it is the circumstance of losing one or both parents and not the specific ordinal position which brought about the alcoholism of the youngest child.

Since it rather frequently happens that a youngest child is born many years after his next youngest sibling, we are often able to observe the ways in which he develops as a kind of compromise between only child and youngest child—and oldest child. At one time this gap of years between last child and previous child was attributed to his being a "change-of-life-baby." More recently he has seemed to make his way upon the scene because of remarriage of a man to a much younger woman who adds a baby to those already on the scene from the man's previous marriage! Whatever the reason for his existence, he is likely to experience considerable pressure and attention from his parents and to identify strongly with them. At the same time, he is likely to be more relaxed, more receptive than his oldest sibling because he receives intervention with the rules, regulations, and restrictions of his parents from a set of surrogate parents: his older siblings. Such a youngest child may have the best of all the positions of oldest, only, and youngest. He is likely to be disciplined little and in gentle ways because his parents are older and less inclined to use physical punishment. He may receive the most sensible guidance and direction by his older siblings who eagerly and delightedly, as very young parent substitutes, take him over and offer him the pleasures they felt they were not accorded by their parents. These older siblings are somewhat like doting grandparents. They have all the joys of parenthood without the stress, tension and responsibilities of actual parenthood. These older siblings are likely to give their youngest sibling all the financial aid possible.

The sex of the youngest child and the sex of siblings help determine how he will experience his role as youngest.

If the youngest child is the only male in the family, he may experience some problems in establishing an adequate masculine identification, neither too extremely masculine nor too weak. The surplus of feminine models in his life may push him in the direction of somewhat feminine identification. An adult homosexual male complained angrily that he could not possibly have developed otherwise because he had four older sisters who smothered him with mothering, but who suppressed his every attempt to be aggressive.

In a family of three girls and a boy, the two younger children were forced by household circumstances to share a room. The boy experienced much hostile physical aggression from his older sister with whom he shared the room. Between his third to seventh years he had an immature speech pattern and many feminine interests. Since his father was away from home a great deal, the boy had little opportunity to learn boys' interests until he entered public school. The persons who served as his most constant models were all females.

If a father is authoritarian and dominant and the mother is kind and doting, a youngest child who is the only boy may line himself up with the father as far as identification is concerned but be very dependent emotionally on women. He will deny the importance of women, but in adulthood he is very likely to remain attached to one in a highly dependent way.

Although the older sisters of an only boy may "mother" him to distraction, the older brothers of an only girl are not likely to overindulge her. They are more likely to avoid her as much as possible and to be disdainful of her attempts to join their activities. If she lives in an area where she has many female playmates outside her home, she is fortunate. But circumstances sometimes force her into close association with her brothers. A busy farm mother with five sons and a single last daughter required the boys to be responsible for the little girl as she played around the farm acres. Her older brothers were relatively tolerant of her because the family as a whole was warm and loving. But the girl grew up feeling inadequate because she had become aware that she could not share their activities with them and she felt herself to be a burden to them. She learned that a scream and a howl would bring immediate attention from her concerned but busy parents. Even a record of straight A's on her report card did not make up for the fact that she could not play baseball as well as they did.

In previous chapters we have said that the oldest child in the family usually achieves better school records and a higher level of education than later-born children. However, in a family of four or more children, the youngest child may achieve more along those lines than the oldest child in such families. In larger families, as we have seen, the one or two older children may be required to assume practical responsibilities for the family while they are still very young. Their education may be interfered with by these responsibilities. The financial resources of the family may be concentrated on the younger children and particularly on the youngest child. In one extremely impoverished family of eight children, the three oldest children left home at an early age and two of them have never been heard from by any member of the family. Two of the middle children assumed care of the three youngest while both parents worked in order to pay for food and shelter. By the time the youngest child was ready to attend high school she was able to do so with some assurance of financial support because the middle children were then earning something to add to the family income. She was the only member of the family to complete high school.

Thus we find that the size of the family may have a great deal to do with the way the youngest child experiences his role. Dr. Bossard[8] found that the youngest children from families of six or more children expressed the greatest degree of adult satisfaction with their childhood role as youngest. One of the findings in a study of the adjustment of illiterate soldiers was that among those coming from families of ten or more children, the last born tended to be better adjusted than earlier born siblings.[9]

REFERENCES

1. HENRY, ANDREW F.: Sibling structure and perception of the disciplinary role of parents. *Sociometry, 20*:67-74, 1957.
2. PALMER, ROBERT D.: Birth order and identification. *J Consult Psychol, 30*:129-135, 1966.
3. BORING, EDWIN G.: *Psychologist at Large.* New York, Basic Books, 1961.
4. CUSHNA, BRUCE; GREENE, MITCHELL, and SNIDER, BILL C. F.: First born and last born children in a child development clinic. *J Individ Psychol, 20*:179-182, 1964.
5. FARINA, AMERIGO; BARRY, HERBERT, III, and GARMEZY, NORMAN: Birth order of recovered and nonrecovered schizophrenics. *Arch Gen Psychiat, 9*:224-228, 1963.

6. BAKAN, D.: The relationship between alcoholism and birth rank. *Quart J Stud Alchol, 10*:434-440, 1949.

7. DE LINT, JAN E. E.: Alcoholism, birth order, and socializing agents. *J Abnor Soc Psychol, 69*:457-458, 1964.

8. BOSSARD, JAMES H. S.: *The Large Family System.* Phil., U of Pa Pr, 1956, p. 203.

9. ALTUS, WILLIAM DAVID: Birth order, intelligence, and adjustment. *Psychol Rep, 5*:502, 1959.

Chapter XIV

THE YOUNGEST CHILD IN ADULTHOOD

PERHAPS achievement, as beauty has been said to do, depends upon the eye of the beholder. If achievement along "worldly" lines is to be our concern, the evidence suggests that the oldest child of four or fewer children is more likely than the youngest child to achieve academic success and eminence in later life. In larger families it is possible, according to the study by Dr. Bossard, that middle children may be more likely than either youngest or oldest children to achieve satisfactory adjustment.

Clinical observation of many cases suggests that the youngest child is more likely than the oldest child to be comfortable in his adult adjustment when both have come from the family of smaller size. Dr. Bossard found that the youngest child from families of six or more children tended to look back with more satisfaction on his role than his siblings did on theirs. His general adult adjustment, however, tended to be less adequate than that of the middle children from these large families.[1]

It is possible that the traditional emphasis society has placed on the position of the oldest child has tended to limit opportunities for the youngest children in families. Youngest sons, for instance, have been found to be in unduly small proportions among medical students,[2] which suggests that family resources may be more readily available to the first son in the family. Now that the prevailing attitude is that all children should be given advanced education who can absorb it, we may find larger proportions of youngest children in college populations and, hence, larger numbers among the adults who have distinguished themselves through academic or professional achievement.

There are special conditions which seem to grow out of the role of youngest in the family which may sometimes seem to limit achievement. Occasionally a youngest child will seem to be so intent upon being like admired older siblings that he will not develop in full his own capabilities and individuality. His basic dissatisfaction with the occupational role he has chosen to fit into the family pattern may show itself in many ways, including an inability to achieve at a high level. One young man from the middle east complained of heart palpitations, easy susceptibility to strange "skin diseases," and tremendous loss of weight. He had become a kind of world wanderer, unable to settle down anywhere. He offered as a reason for his wandering that he was the one the family had chosen to represent their business interests around the world. But even they were concerned about the length of time he stayed away from his home country and the occasional business errors he made. After he had come to accept his real dislike for the business activities in which his older brothers had such success he was able to move into the law career he really wanted. His physical symptoms soon waned and so did his urge to be forever on the move.

The female youngest child is usually well able to accept financial dependency when she is an adult. Her usual preference is for the role of housewife and mother and she is willing to permit her husband to be the one who has the career and who supports the household financially.

The adult youngest child is often a most pleasant companion, one with whom it is possible to relax and enjoy oneself. Out of their childhood position sometimes develops, however, a propensity for quick flare-ups of anger. The source of these is often found to be teasing or other pressure from older siblings. I was, for instance, standing in a line with other women at a school luncheon when a very charming acquaintance of mine suddenly flared up and said, "Don't do that!" when another woman tried, by tugging at her arm, to move her into another position. Several of us were startled by the speaker's intensity and she laughed and explained, "I was the youngest of eight children and I can't stand it when people use physical force to move me about!"

In adulthood the youngest child may be quite adept at using devious ways of bringing other people to conform to his wishes. A female youngest child complained that she was not sure any more that she "knew what the truth was" because she had so completely adopted a ruse of telling people what she thought would keep them comfortable with her, rather than that which might require her to defend her stand. She called for help when she found herself rather firmly engaged to two men and felt that she "couldn't possibly" clear up the issue because the one she didn't want to marry "might be angry or hurt."

Youngest children are likely to accept leadership and authority with comfort because they have learned ways of getting what they want without coming into direct conflict with authority. On the other hand, if, in childhood, they were required to defend themselves a great deal or were placed in the position of controlling the older ones because they were youngest, they may be quite imperious and demanding in adulthood. Such reactions have particularly been seen in youngest children who were the only representatives of their sex in the family; i.e., followed a line of siblings of the opposite sex. Both a male youngest and a female youngest may then become quite commanding.

The female youngest child is likely to seek out friends who are older than she. Since they allow her to continue her role of being "the baby," she is comfortable with them. She is likely to place great importance on the specific number of years between her and other people. One female youngest child commented with great satisfaction, "I'm the baby in this group." She and her friends were all on the "mature" side of fifty! Another youngest child invariably announces that her older sister is "over eighty." The implication, of course, is that she is much younger, say seventy-five! Older sister's good-natured comment is, "It takes a babbling brook of a little sister to tell one's age!"

The youngest child is not likely to remain unmarried. Dr. Walter Toman[3] found a tendency for youngest children to select mates who had been the oldest child or the oldest of the middle children in their families. The youngest brothers of brothers tended to marry oldest sisters.

The youngest child, however, will not necessarily be happiest in a marriage to an older or oldest child, because he or she may feel quite dominated by the spouse. Occasionally a youngest child will seem quite willing to be subjugated by a spouse who will take advantage of them in many ways but who give them the feeling of being a "child" in relation to them. A young woman was so dominated by her oldest child husband that even after they were divorced and the process servers were trying to find him to serve papers she consented, after meeting him accidentally, to go to his apartment with him. And she submitted to being blindfolded by him so that she wouldn't be able to tell the process servers where he was staying!

The female youngest child will often marry a man who is considerably older than she. She will then be able to retain the role of "child." The male youngest child is not likely to marry a woman who is older than he; it is rather easy to associate such a relationship with the domination of the older females in the family.

A close relationship or marriage between a man and a woman who were both youngest children can become a subtle but persistent tug of war to see who will get the most care and the largest share of good things. A male youngest child who had met his wife in high school commented, "It seemed to me even then that each of us was always grabbing for the attention that comes to the youngest in the family."

When there is a sufficient supply of very good things to keep both people contented, a marriage between two younger or youngest children has the possibility of being most enjoyable. One famous younger sister married to a youngest child says that the two of them act like teen-agers. Elizabeth Taylor described her attitude toward both her older brother and toward Richard Burton as one of complete faith and adoration.[4]

It is very important for the youngest child to continue to feel loved and cherished by the spouse. Having learned in childhood that the affection and protection of the older siblings were very important because they ensured that the youngest would receive the good things he wanted and needed, the youngest tends to remain dependent on the good will of the other people in his environment for security. Maurice Chevalier, the youngest of three brothers, says that his happiness depends upon his being "in love" and that he is "in love" when he is loved.[5]

A female youngest child may annoy her husband by not assuming some of the household responsibilities. She may both dislike them and be little skilled in doing them because older siblings took care of these things for her. An oldest sister who had just been a visitor in the home of her youngest sister commented, "She treats him just the way my mother who was a youngest sister always treated my father. She won't cook for him. The apartment is a mess. He has to take care of his own clothes, taking them to the cleaners and all that sort of thing."

Everything may be very sunny in the marriage of the youngest child as long as there is no great frustration of the needs of the spouse who is youngest child. When frustration does occur, the youngest child may allow the "little child within" to take over and become petulant and irritable. As the youngest child moves from childhood to adulthood, there is likely to remain a strong feeling for the importance of the role of being a child among other people. A young wife commented about her husband who had been the youngest of four: "He doesn't want to grow up. He acts like a little boy. He seems to be saying 'Please love me because I'm a cute little kid.' "

The greatest challenge to the adult adjustment of the youngest child may be that of parenthood. The youngest child often seems surprised to find himself a "grown-up person" with responsibilities of home, spouse, and children. One male youngest child said that he had a great shock one Sunday afternoon as he stood in his front yard watering the lawn. "I looked around," he said, "and I had the sudden thought: 'Believe it or not, all this belongs to me—*Little Arnold!*' "

A new mother, youngest of five children, left her baby in a carriage in front of a store one day and completely forgot about him for several hours! Fortunately, when she finally recollected that she had lost something, she found him where she left him, still sound asleep! "I've always had people looking for me," she said. "Now I'll have to start looking after someone else."

Like the only child, the youngest child may sometimes compete with the children for the attention of the spouse. A woman, who had several older sisters, obviously managed contacts between her husband and their daughter so that he did not give the child a great deal of time or companionship.

REFERENCES

1. BOSSARD, JAMES H. S.: *The Large Family System.* Phil., U of Pa Pr, 1956, p. 255.

2. COBB, SIDNEY, and FRENCH, JOHN R., JR.: Birth order among medical students. *JAMA, 195*:312-313, 1966.

3. TOMAN, WALTER: Choices of marriage partners by men coming from monosexual sibling configurations. *Brit J Med Psychol, 37*:43-46, 1964.

4. TAYLOR, ELIZABETH: *Elizabeth Taylor, An Informal Memoir.* New York, Avon Books, 1967.

5. CHEVALIER, MAURICE: *With Love.* Boston, Little, 1960.

Chapter XV

SUGGESTIONS TO PARENTS AND TO PEOPLE WHO INTEND TO BE PARENTS

SOMEDAY, perhaps, we shall understand so fully the conditions which bring about a certain human personality and behavioral make-up that we shall be able to computerize parenthood. We shall say: "Push that button, synchronize those adjustments, and there you are—the kind of child you would like to have."

But now we don't know. We neither know the conditions which will in their entirety and combination bring about a particular result, nor are we ready to control the environment so that it will produce the necessary conditions. But many of us are constantly searching for causes and slowly more information seems to be available to us.

We do have evidence, though, that all living creatures respond in their development to the external circumstances of their environment, and that the conditions which surround them in their early formative years have a lasting influence. We have said in this book that the early environment of the child must be considered to contain more than the parents. The fact that the child has brothers and sisters or none must be taken into account. It has been claimed that they influence his development through constant social interaction with him. It has also been claimed that the way his parents and siblings react to him is largely determined by the position he holds among them: whether he is oldest, middle, youngest, only.

We have not claimed that the position the child holds in his family will make him into a genius or an idiot, nor do we claim that his entire personality or character will be molded by the circumstances of his birth order. We have said that the position he holds among his siblings will allow him to use some of his inherited attributes in certain ways. He may seem more verbal or intellectual at an earlier age because he is stimulated by his siblings to use his intelligence. But the effect of birth order on the individual seems to develop mainly out of the role he plays as a result of his position in the family and how it causes him to interact socially with other members of the family. He is usually relatively different from the other members of the family. In a family where responsibility is stressed by the parents, all members of the family are likely to be responsible. But, because parents tend to place greater pressure for responsibility on the first child in the family, that oldest child is likely to be the most responsible of the siblings.

Thus we in no way take away from the parents the final responsibility for the personalities and characters of their children. It is they who are the models for the kind of approaches their children will take to each other. If parents are kind, tolerant, calm people, all of their children are likely to show these characteristics. But, because of his birth position, the oldest child is likely to be relatively more tense and quick to be angered than any of his siblings. But if he is to be compared with the oldest child of angry, disciplining parents, he will display the influence of his family environment and be relatively tolerant and calm.

It must also be stressed that the effects described as having a certain place in the family are in no way fixed and inevitable. They only tend to occur in our society because families in our society usually follow a certain general pattern. A most important reason for describing what so often occurs is to alert parents to the things they must do to ensure that their children avoid the problems which might arise out of being in the various birth order positions.

It is also hoped that the information given in this book will help to allay some of the anxieties of parents and help them to be relatively relaxed and comfortable in the highly responsible job of raising children. You should not feel that you have somehow failed if your first child gives evidence of jealousy when the second arrives. Perhaps what has been said will help you to tolerate his jealousy because it is so inevitable in most situations. When your middle child complains that he feels neglected, perhaps you can console yourself with the possibility that he is also learning to be adaptable to many kinds of people: those older and those younger; those who must be aided and directed and those who will be in authority over him.

Consider, too, the influence of your own birth order on your way of being a parent. Do you, as oldest child, tend to be more authoritarian than is comfortable in the family? Or, as youngest child, would you like your children to "baby" you?

Another consideration is that of the way your birth order interacts with those of your children. Are you, as oldest child, in conflict with your own oldest child because both you and he would like to be in charge of situations and tell the other what to do? As youngest child are you perhaps a bit competitive with your own youngest child for any indulgences that might be available?

Here are listed in summary form some of the ways the birth order of your child may influence your relationship with him and his development as child and adult:

1. The birth order of each child in your family may cause you to react somewhat differently to each of them. Your expectations, your discipline, the closeness of your relationship with him will vary somewhat with each child according to his birth order.

2. Your own birth order will influence to some extent your general ways of being parental.

3. Your own birth order will have something to do with the way you react to each child according to his birth order. As oldest, you may come in conflict with your own oldest, etc.

4. Each child in your family will view you in a different way according to his birth order. His birth order will determine to some extent the degree to which you are a model for him and the intensity of his wish for closeness with you.

5. The children in your family will react to each other in many ways that will depend upon the birth order of each of them.

6. Your knowledge and understanding of birth order influences will make it possible for you to adjust conditions so that possibly adverse effects can be avoided.

As we went along, we have suggested many ways to put birth order information to use in the job of raising children. We will now attempt to provide the further emphasis and explanation which some of the suggestions may require.

The Two-Child Family

Experts consistently advise that parents of a two-child family should take care to recognize the different developmental levels of their children and give them frequent opportunities for separate activity.

Some of the intense and occasionally uncomfortable emotional interaction among the four members of the two-child family seems to be due to a tendency for them all to be in close contact so much of the time. The two children, especially if they are somewhat close in age, are often expected by their parents to be constant companions. It is sometimes difficult to remember that even only a year's difference in age can make quite a difference in physical strength, intellectual capacity, and general interests. If the age difference between them is less than four years, they are likely to be quite competitive with each other. And, of course, any two human beings who are together a great deal can be expected to clash wills occasionally.

It has been suggested, then, that the two children be provided with separate play situations during some portion of each day. Parents who live in neighborhoods where there are many other children may find that their children may quite naturally seek separate playmates and so accomplish their own separation. Other parents may find it necessary to make special arrangements to meet their childrens' different interests.

It is also suggested that parents bring right out into the open their recognition of the differences between their two children in terms of age and sex. If older sister Kate makes fun of younger sister Bianca's attempts to do anything which her older sister can do better, a parent may remark, "Bianca has to learn, just as Kate did at her age." Such a casual remark soothes Bianca's pride and encourages her to keep on trying. At the same time it tells Kate that her parent is aware that she can do better, but she must remember that being older helps to make it possible.

The Boy-Boy Family

Although all parents must be prepared to have their children display competitiveness and jealousy from time to time, the parents of only two boys may be often challenged to remain calm and understanding.

It is all very well for experts to dispense the advice that, upon the birth of a younger child, parents must make every effort to see that the older child receives even more attention than he previously received. Parents are human beings and they are limited in the strength and time which they can devote to each of two children. Recently I read a suggestion that Mother should make use of the time she has while the baby is napping to play with her older child. What I wonder is how she then gets around to doing the dishes and dusting the furniture, to say nothing of cleaning up the general disorder two small children make and preparing Daddy's dinner. And when does she find a little time to rest so that she has the energy to go from 6 A.M. bottle time to 10 P.M. bottle time?

I think part of the answer lies in careful management of the older boy's time and activities. He needs interesting toys so that he is kept occupied. It is extremely important that he have a play space outdoors where he is safe and Mother can relax without worry while he is outside. Mothers, too, can often find some relaxation and rest if they and their children spend some time every day with other mothers with small children. A childless woman commented to me that the young mothers in her housing complex tended to do nothing all afternoon but sit outside on the grass gossiping with neighbors and "watching their children grow." She didn't know, not yet having had the experience herself, that the young women were getting much needed rest between chores and their children were being kept busy and contented and well supervised.

Each of your two boys needs to have your assistance in helping him avoid any special problems that might go along with his place in the family as older or younger brother. The older boy needs to be protected from the anger and tension he feels when he is excessively criticized or parents insist upon more adult and independent behavior than can be expected at his age. He is likely, anyway, to be constantly striving to live up to your standards and to be as much like you as possible. In trying to be "parental" he may even seem "bossy" and it may seem to you sometimes that he is trying to compete with you as the authority. Help him to relax. Tell him to calm down when he gets tense and anxious. Physical expression of affection can be very reassuring at times and you are lucky if your child welcomes a comforting pat on the shoulder or a tight hug when he seems all wound up. Let him know, as he gets older, that he has a right and a need as a human being to spend part of his time doing activities that are simply enjoyable.

The older child may sometimes need reassurance that he does not always have to achieve at a high level; that anyone who tries to do anything at all is expected to make some mistakes.

The younger boy needs to be encouraged to be as independent and mature as his age level permits at any one time. Parents should not encourage babyish qualities in either speech or behavior. He should be asked to assume responsibilities just as is his older brother.

Parents may need to be alert to the possibility that the younger boy can sometimes use subtle means of getting his older brother into trouble. He may learn at a very early age to manipulate situations so that it seems to be only the older boy who is causing problems in the home. The older boy is likely to be rather direct in the way he expresses hostility and competitiveness. He may use his superior strength and push and hit or take a toy away from his brother. Younger brother's maneuvers are likely to be more artful. He may not grab a toy from the other child; instead he may hide it when no one is looking.

It is important for the development of both boys that you require the younger one to do his fair share of chores, taking as much responsibility at his level of ability as the older boy does at his.

The Girl-Girl Family

Parents of the two-girl family may want to keep in mind that the younger of two girls may feel herself to be very much at a disadvantage in competing with her older sister. Her sister tends to receive the approval of the parents because of her more mature behavior. Younger sister may then react by being hostile and negativistic. Parents, then, will want to encourage the younger girl to develop her own interests and skills and not press her to compete with her sister. She very much needs approval of her accomplishments at her own level of ability.

Mothers sometimes tend to spend more time with their first

child than with the second one and this can mean that the younger daughter does not have much opportunity to learn feminine skills and to identify with her mother. Both girls need to share activities with their mother.

The older of two daughters has a tendency to overdo being a "good girl" so that she can please her parents and compete successfully with younger sister in holding their love and attention. If the parents are themselves driving and perfectionistic, they may inadvertently place too much pressure on that older girl to be "perfect" and thus cause her to be tense and uncomfortable. The parents may find themselves better able to relax their standards if they keep in mind that the older daughter's tendency is usually to achieve at the very highest level possible to please them.

The Girl-Boy Family

It is important for the mother of this family to understand that the presence of a brother may be especially disturbing to the older sister; she will be helped a great deal by a close, warm relationship with her mother. She needs to be reassured that the birth of a brother does not in any way lose her the love of her parents and that being a girl does not somehow make her less valuable to them than her brother is. Since many parents, consciously or unconsciously, have quite special feelings about their sons, this reassurance may be difficult to give. Being aware of the problem, however, will help parents to say and do things that will alleviate some of their daughter's anxiety. When brother is first born, she may be allowed to help mother with some of his care. As time goes on, her accomplishments along feminine lines need to be approved.

The daughter's tendency on the birth of a brother is to turn away from mother and toward father for comfort and companionship. It will be well if her father is gentle with her, but he should also limit the amount of time he spends with her. It is preferable that she continue to be companionable with her mother.

On the other hand, it is very important that the father become companionable with his son as early as possible so that the influence of two older females (mother and sister) will not be too important in the development of the boy. In fact, it is just as well if the situation ends up with a kind of coalition between sexes in the family: mother and daughter on one side and father and son on the other.

The Boy-Girl Family

The parents of the boy-girl family may consider themselves fortunate. It is this family which usually seems to be the most comfortable to raise.

Sometimes one or both parents will feel a strong preference for the boy, the first and only son. Obviously, then, their daughter will suffer feelings of rejection and inadequacy unless they make every effort to recognize her special qualities and come to value those.

A particular complaint of many girls in such two-child families is that brother is not required to do nearly as much in the way of household chores as his sister is. Obviously, both children should have responsibilities given to them.

The Only Child

Perhaps the most useful suggestion that can be given to the parent of an only child is to relax! There is no need to be more concerned about him than any parent has to be about a child. He has special problems, but so does any child in growing up. And, like any other child, there are certain advantages connected with his position in the family.

In the chapter on the childhood of the only child some of the special conditions which may beset him were mentioned, as were remedies for these conditions.

The parents of the only child have a tendency to concentrate a great proportion of their own time and energy on him. It is better, usually, if they do not over emphasize this. The mother of an only child does not need to give as much time to mothering as does the mother of more children, and it will be better for her and for her child if she finds outside interests and activities.

It seems desirable in most cases for an only child to be raised in a neighborhood where there are many possible playmates so that he need not be alone too much.

The parents of only children often try to keep their child from feeling alone on family expeditions by inviting other children along. This is often a very good thing to do, but it sometimes seems to the only child to be overdone. The reason is that the child sometimes interprets it as an attempt on his parents' part to exclude him from the parental relationship. Children also enjoy feeling that their parents like to have their companionship. The one-child family may have only three members, but to the child it is "his family" and like other children he will much appreciate those times when the "whole family" does things as a unit.

I should like to suggest that the parents of only children read the book *The Only Child* by Norma E. Cutts and Nicholas Moseley.[1] Although it was published in 1954 and at this time is out of print, it is available in libraries. It is informative and, of considerable importance for the parents of an Only Child, reassuring.

The Oldest Child

The ways of being "parental" include the manner in which authority is exercised and the approach taken by the parent in imposing his standards on his child. Fulfilling the parental role is likely to engage the more serious, conscientious, and disciplining aspects of the personality of a mother or father. The parent is more likely to show to another adult the potentialities he has for relaxation or dependency than he is to show these in the relationship with his child.

Thus the oldest child is likely to receive the full impact of the sterner aspects of the parents' personalities. Since this pressure may make him uncomfortable, he is likely to react in ways that will make his parents uncomfortable. It is suggested, then, that the parents of oldest children take a good look at their own behavior and then a second look at the behavior of their first-borns. They are very likely to find that the two behavior patterns are quite similar.

If a parent finds his oldest child easily irritated, angry, overly assertive or authoritative in his relations with others, the parent might consider whether or not his own approach toward his child errs in these directions. If he wants his oldest child to be tolerant, patient and kind, he usually has only to adopt these ways of behaving himself and he will eventually find his oldest child to be using them.

The parent of an oldest child will want to understand the special adjustments which that child has to make because of his place in the family hierarchy, and that he will almost inevitably display somewhat alarming behavior from time to time. He is trying to come to terms with frustrations and responsibilities which are often specific to his family position. If his family environment is within usual limits with no extremes of tension or violence or other pathological conditions, he is very likely to develop eventually into a capable and responsible human being.

If you are interested in reading more about the first-born child, you will find *The Eldest Child* by Edith G. Neisser[2] most informative.

The Middle Child

The parents of three children may be more in need of assistance in guiding their one middle child than the parents of a larger number of children. There are two circumstances which seem to be especially traumatic to the adjustment of the middle child. One is to be the middle child of three children of the same sex, and the other is to be the only male among the three children.

If the middle child is one of three children of the same sex, he may develop along one of two very different lines. He may become very unlike his siblings or he may, on the other hand, seem to subordinate his personality to theirs. An example of the first adjustment was a middle girl who was caught shop lifting. She had taken a few inexpensive items and the store detective considered it necessary to report her delinquency only to her parents and, fortunately, not to outside authorities. The parents obtained counseling for themselves and for their daughter. They learned that she had felt deprived of their attention and love and that they had been giving much more attention to their oldest and youngest daughters, who were not only in birth order positions which favored this, but who were also achieving at higher levels in school. Deprived of the gratification of her parent's approval, she turned, as do so many preadolescent or adolescent children, to thefts of small things which would give her pleasure. Her parents began to give her more time and attention and, more important perhaps, formulated plans for a program that would enhance her development. She was tutored in her weakest school subjects and enrolled in art lessons at a local museum. Five years later she is a relatively contented young woman who is planning to start a business course in the fall.

The middle child of three children of the same sex may withdraw from any suggestion of independent behavior. The parents of a nine-year-old middle child were alarmed by his seeming lack of interest in any activities other than those in which he could accompany his older or younger brother. He seemed interested only in taking part in their activities and to develop none of his own. The parents found that he concentrated on being with his brothers because he had little close contact with either parent. His only emotional security lay in companionship with his brothers. Like most children he responded readily to a parental change in attitude. All that was needed in this case was special attention. Concrete evidence of their concern through their making plans for him soon made him a much more independent person as well as a more emotionally comfortable boy.

In a preceding chapter there was some discussion of the problems that might arise for the boy who is the middle child with an older and younger sister. It was then suggested that it is very important for the father of a boy in such a situation to make a special effort to develop a close relationship with him. It would not be unsatisfactory, in fact, if the boy and his dad formed a kind a coalition against the female contingent in the family.

The parents of larger families may take comfort in the possibility that their middle children are developing rather comfortably and in the direction of relatively good adult adjustment. The child who might most need their special attention could be a second child, who is the first son in the family. Although they may take special pride in him because he is the first boy, he is very likely to feel strongly competitive with the older sister. Both Ernest Hemingway,[3] the renowned writer, and the son of Charlie Chaplin, Michael,[4] were the second children and first sons in large families. According to published accounts, both boys were highly competitive with their older sisters. This competition seems to have had an effect on Michael that was highly destructive to his self-esteem, while it only stimulated Hemingway to sharper intellectual efforts. It seems to me that the effect of the competition in each case may have depended a great deal upon the boy's relationship with his father. Throughout Michael's account of his first nineteen years there seems to me to be a constant mourning for the lack of close contact with his father. Ernest Hemingway went with his father on his medical calls; they had an extremely close relationship. Out of such examples grows the suggestion that the second child who is the first son in the family may need a close relationship with his father for many reasons, but that one of these reasons is development and support of his masculinity in competition with the female who is in a dominant position as oldest sister.

The parents of a family of five or more children will want to be aware that occasionally a child will seek status along lines that give him special attention and help him stand out in the crowd, but that are inimical to good future adjustment. Dr. Bossard,[5] whose study of the large family has previously been recommended, lists as some of the unfavorable roles that children may assume in large families: those of being the family isolate or the irresponsible one of the family or the sickly one. We might add to the list the one who is delinquent or physically aggressive or overly passive. The parent will be fortunate if he stops development along such lines at an early stage. This he will be able to do only if he becomes informed about the possibilities and remains alert to the changes in development of each of his children. Since all of this requires a great deal of time and attention on the part of both parents, it is good that the parents of large families, especially those in the middle or upper classes, seem to have their large families by design, not chance. The father as well as the mother usually seems quite willing to share responsibilities for everyday care of the children.

The Youngest Child

The relationship between the older children in the family and the youngest child should be controlled so that either of two conditions is avoided. First, the older children should not be allowed to treat the youngest as though he is a kind of toy. This is sometimes a subtle ruse on the part of the older children to keep the youngest in an inferior position. It ensures that he will then have no active or important part in the family's affairs. The second condition to be avoided is too much domination of the youngest by the older children. If they are physically aggressive toward him, he may either withdraw into excessive passivity or become violently and angrily defensive. If their domination takes the form of "bossiness," he will not learn to be independent.

Youngest children sometimes become quite defensive and quick-tempered because they are teased a great deal by their elders. While teasing may have over-tones of being relatively socially acceptable, it is generally only a cover-up for a hostile attempt to irritate the other person. For a child who is younger and smaller and therefore relatively defenseless, it can be experienced as a very real and frightening attack. Many youngest children are, as adults, distrustful of others because they were much teased as children.

On the other hand, parents will want to discourage any tendency on the part of the youngest child to control his older siblings by excessive complaining and tattling. If you always accept his word for the misbehavior of his siblings, they are likely to feel that you are unfair and to dislike the youngest child. The youngest needs to know that you will listen to his complaints, but that you will also insist upon knowing the other side of the story from his sibling.

The youngest child needs encouragement and support in learning to participate in activities with others outside the home. Since he is the youngest, both his parents and he will sometimes be reluctant to push outside activities. His parents do not have the motivation they had with the older children; they no longer need to be left free to care for younger children. They may also wish to keep him a baby as long as possible, which is exactly the opposite of what they wanted for the oldest. But remaining immature is all too easy for the youngest; he must be encouraged to grow up.

It has been mentioned that the youngest is more likely than the other children to experience the loss of one or both parents. If this should happen to a child, the adults remaining responsible for him should not try to protect him by withholding information from him. His questions should be answered in such a way that he receives just the information he requires at the moment—no more, no less. As when the parent teaches the child about sexual matters, it must not be assumed that the child needs the detailed information that an adult requires for full understanding. He does, however, need to know enough of the facts so that his lively childish imagination does not distort the situation. He must come to understand, for instance, that he is not personally responsible for the separation or divorce of parents or for the illness or death of one or both. It is important, too, that he be allowed to express his feelings. If any extreme or long-lasting symptoms occur, such as sleeplessness, nightmares, reverting to earlier forms of behavior such as wetting or soiling, professional help should be sought.

REFERENCES

1. Cutts, Norma E., and Moseley, Nicholas: *The Only Child.* New York, Putnam, 1954.
2. Neisser, Edith G.: *The Eldest Child.* New York, Harper, 1957.
3. Hemingway, Leicester: *My Brother, Ernest Hemingway.* New York, Fawcett, 1967.
4. Chaplin, Michael: *I Couldn't Smoke the Grass on My Father's Lawn.* New York, Ballantine, 1966.
5. Bossard, James H. S.: *The Large Family System: An Original Study in the Sociology of Family Behavior.* Phil., U of Pa Pr, 1956.

Chapter XVI

ADDITIONAL SUGGESTIONS FOR ADULTS ACCORDING TO THEIR BIRTH ORDER

IN THE previous chapters various suggestions have been given concerning problems to be met in raising children according to their birth order and the tendencies of adult development have been described. Reference has been made to marital and occupational adjustments which might or might not be suitable or expected according to the position of the person in the family hierarchy. In this chapter I shall enumerate some of the most important considerations for persons raised in the various birth order positions.

For Adults Who Grew Up in Two-Child Families

The Man Who Was the Older Son in a Boy-Boy Family

You have, very likely, acquired from your parents some very strict standards of behavior which you tend to impose on yourself and on other people. You will find it helpful if you try to be more tolerant and patient with yourself as well as with others. Take time for activities that you do just because you enjoy them.

The Man Who Was the Younger Son in a Boy-Boy Family

As a younger brother you may have learned to follow others rather than to take the lead in many situations. You may need to develop more confidence in your ability to take initiative and learn to be aggressive in relating to other people.

It usually is not necessary to suggest to you that you learn to relax and enjoy yourself. Rather you might need to consider whether or not you are striking a proper balance between work and play.

Your position as younger brother very likely helped you develop good skills along athletic lines. You may, however, not have developed your full potentialities in verbal skills even though you may have achieved a high level of professional or occupational status. If further progress depends upon more education or making better speeches or writing more adequate letters, take steps to develop these verbal skills.

The Woman Who Was the Older of Two Daughters

The suggestions for the man who was an older brother may be applicable in your case.

Although we usually think of sibling rivalry as a condition involving children, this is not always true. Adult brothers and sisters are also susceptible to jealousy and competitiveness, and the older of two sisters is often quite vulnerable to these feelings. Older sister can rather easily compete with little sister when both are children or adolescents, but the situation may change as they grow older. The family position of the younger girl tends to make her into the kind of person who attracts an aggressive male. Hence she may make a very good marriage and her adult adjustment may rival in comfort that of her older sister. Like any other adult sibling, older sister will need to recognize that she must accept little sister as an equal and as another adult with a life quite separate from hers.

The Woman Who Was the Younger of Two Daughters

The suggestions for the man who grew up as a younger brother may apply to you also, so please refer back to them.

Usually the girl who is raised as the younger of two sisters is most in need of help and reassurance when she is an adolescent or young adult. It is then that she may suffer the effects of having an older sister who seems to outdo her in so many ways. It is important, then, that you develop your own interests and abilities rather than attempting to compete with your sister in areas in which she may excel. Do not be discouraged by the fact that she achieves success in so many ways before you do. It is only natural that she should do this because she is older than you and more emotionally mature at any one time during adolescence and young adulthood.

Do not expect to be like her. Allow yourself to develop as the separate individual you are and it is very likely that you will be able to achieve fully as much as she in adulthood.

The Woman Who Was the Older Sister of a Brother

You may need to temper any tendencies you have to dominate and compete with males. Since you are likely to be competent and aggressive along verbal lines, you may see as less adequate males who tend not to be so verbal. Consequently, men may be a bit cautious about establishing close relationships with you because of the challenge to their own self-respect. In the chapter on the specific kinds of two-child families, some recommendations have been made for wives who grew up as older sisters of brothers.

The Man Who Was the Younger Brother of a Sister

The family position in which you grew up may have caused you to be somewhat more sensitive to feminine needs than a man might be who grew up in another family position. You may tend to be less outwardly aggressive, too. This may mean that you would make a very comfortable marital partner for most women, but a girl friend or wife who is herself aggressive might consider that you are not being as masculine or aggressive as she might like. Make sure that she reads what was said about men who grew up as younger brothers of sisters so she will see that she must learn to relax and trust you as the responsible person you are.

The Man Who Was the Older Brother of a Sister

Perhaps the most important thing for you to learn is to be tolerant and understanding of the opposite sex. Since you were older and stronger than your sister in most cases, you are likely to be somewhat disdainful of what you may view as weaknesses in females. Consequently, girl friends and wives may consider you thoughtless and overly demanding at times. However, like Pablo Picasso who also grew up in this family position,[1] you may find many women ready to admire and serve your masculine aggressiveness.

The Woman Who Was the Younger Sister of a Brother

The most trying time in your life may be the point at which you must take financial responsibility for yourself. If you do not find a suitable marriage partner who will supply you with emotional and financial security, you may flounder a bit before you select a suitable career. It will be necessary for you to overcome some of the passivity that may have developed as the result of having been a female younger child, who identified rather strongly with a mother who probably was a housewife rather than a careerist.

The Adult Only Child

Allow yourself to be proud of the special advantages you had as an only child. Do not permit yourself or other people to tell you that you are "spoiled" unless you really are! Being "spoiled" can mean many different things and I am not sure what they are and whether or not they are accurate. I assume that some of the meanings can be that the individual asks too much of other people, is not concerned with the needs of other people, and is not appreciative of what other people do for him. The only child may need to make sure that he is not making *giving* a one-way street, always from other people to him.

Enjoy your ability to enjoy yourself and other people. Come to terms with your "child within" and learn to accept it and to control it. I highly recommend that you read *Your Inner Child of the Past* by W. Hugh Missildine, M.D.[2] This book will help you understand and put to constructive use that "child within."

Only children often have a special need to appraise realistically their physical health. They can do this by having regular medical examinations and by then accepting whole-heartedly the physician's assurances of their good health, the usual outcome of such examinations. The only child may then need to overlook minor physical discomforts, which might have received the sympathetic attention of his parents, but are unlikely to be accepted by spouses or employers as good reasons for withdrawing from all usual everyday activities.

The Adult Oldest Child

You may find it somewhat difficult to establish and to maintain close, intimate friendships. You may tend to be rather distant in your relationships and to preserve something of the attitudes you took toward your younger siblings. You may strive to feel in charge of others, a bit superior to them. You may resist accepting them as equals and be uncomfortable and somewhat resentful if they do not accept dependency in the relationship with you. You may often drop friendships because you are unconsciously competitive for leadership. You may seek to affiliate with other people so you can be "big brother" or "big sister" rather than share companionship with them. If these ploys make you a more lonely person than you wish to be, you may need to accept the reality of the situation: your adult friends do not wish you to play the role of oldest child with them. They wish to be seen as adults with capabilities equal to yours, with potentialities for aiding you as much as you aid them.

The oldest child may need to examine his relationships with fellow employees and with those who supervise him as well as with those whom he supervises. Is he relating to them as though they are younger siblings to be dominated and controlled? Is he overly stern and exacting with those he supervises? Does he permit them independence of action and development of pride in achievement? Does he covertly rebel against his supervisors as though they are parents with whom to compete rather than other adults with a job to do?

Any oldest child might have a tendency to assume more responsibility than he can handle adequately in terms of available time and energy. Female oldest children are particularly apt to do this. They attempt to raise children, keep house, maintain a social life for themselves and their husbands, and take on responsibilities outside the home such as a job or such demanding volunteer work as being President of the P.T.A. or chairman of a fund drive. The result of such self-driven undertakings is often development of resentment because "other people are forcing" them to do so much. The true cause, of course, is the conscience of the oldest child which says that work and accomplishment must be constantly pursued and relaxation is rather sinful.

As parents, both the male and the female oldest child must nurture in themselves the ability to relax with their children so their homes can resound with laughter and fun as well as with plaudits for achievement. They may need to temper their tendencies to control and dominate their children so that those children will develop independence.

The female oldest child may want to consider carefully certain tendencies which may grow out of her childhood role as big sister and interfere with her adult role as the wife of her husband. She may try to compete with her husband which will make neither of them happy. Even the female oldest child who is a "career woman" will not be happy if she does not consider her husband to be the "man" of the family and that she would be able, if there were need, to depend on him for support and protection. She should be aware that the first role she had in life (and it was the one she always secretly preferred) was that of only child. Deeply hidden beneath the big sister attitude is a wish to have a strong and protective father. Thus she loses both her own feeling of security and her respect for her husband, if she is either successful or thinks she is successful in forcing her husband to take a "little brother" role with her.

She must, therefore, keep clearly in mind the reality of the situation and, especially, make every effort to see her husband as he really is. He is quite likely, unless she seriously erred in her choice of mate, to be a responsible, adequate male who will only be resentful of any female attempt to dominate him and possibly threaten his masculinity. She can be neither big sister nor daughter in the relationship with him; she has to fulfill only the role of wife. Since she grew up as big sister, she is likely to have learned many skills which enable her to be especially strong and supporting in her adult roles and to be a full and equal partner with her husband in their enterprise of marriage.

The Adult Middle Child

The adaptability which the middle child learns as he grows up in a family of some size offers him many adult advantages, as we have seen. He may also develop a tendency to subordinate his own needs to those of others to an extent that sometimes works to his disadvantage. In the interest of serving others, he may fail to develop some of his own potentialities for creativity and successful competition outside the home. The female middle child may find herself, as wife and mother, so involved in meeting the needs of her family that she allows many of her own needs to go unfulfilled.

Middle children, then, may wish to consider the possibility that they have not developed themselves fully as individuals. It may be that some of the problems which arise in their relationships develop out of their tendency to overestimate the importance of the needs of other people. A female middle child complained that her husband wanted her complete attention at all times. She could not leave their home during the daytime, she said, because he might telephone. Since all this attention didn't seem to make her husband comfortable, it was suggested to him that he should insist that his wife develop interests and activities outside the home. He stopped falling in with her need to be needed and they both became more contented with each other. This middle child is an example of the way the needs of the childhood position can impose themselves on an adult situation. This middle child was carrying into the relationship with her husband, her childhood need to have others dependent on her so that she could identify with her parents and her older siblings. In adulthood she ran into trouble because she tried to relate to her husband as though he were a childhood sibling rather than another adult. Like all of us, she needed to adjust her adult behavior to the adult situation.

Since middle children have so often grown to adulthood with some feeling that they were in a relatively unfortunate position in childhood, I suggest that they begin to accept and enjoy the benefits of what was likely to have been a favorable position in the family.

The Adult Youngest Child

If all is well with the youngest child, he may as an adult be enjoyed by other people and be able to enjoy them. He may be able both to give and to receive with great comfort. As youngest child he may have been sufficiently indulged so that he now has an optimistic and out-going point of view.

He may, however, have grown up feeling relatively inadequate in comparison with his older siblings. They and his parents may have encouraged him in the retention of immature ways of behaving and feeling. He may, then, as an adult be unable to overcome frustrations aggressively and independently. Some youngest children find it difficult as adults to take responsibility for other people and even to make decisions that seriously affect their own welfare. They tend to turn to other people for support and help.

The youngest child may need to work on developing a mature point of view and on growing up psychologically as well as physically. It is important for the person who grew up as the "baby" of a family to evaluate carefully his behavior and make sure that he reacts as an adult who is on equal footing with other adults.

One of the special hazards of the youngest child is that he may lose in childhood one or both parents. This loss may occur through separation, divorce of the parents, or as the result of illness or death of one or both. The adult youngest child who has experienced such a loss should understand that it can sometimes have a seriously disturbing effect upon the personality of the child. He should give himself the opportunity, either through careful self-evaluation or with outside professional help, to determine the effect such childhood loss might have had on his development and to alleviate any discomfort he still experiences as the result of the loss.

REFERENCES

1. STEIN, GERTRUDE: *Picasso*, Boston, Beacon, 1959, p. 2.
2. MISSILDINE, W. HUGH: *Your Inner Child of the Past.* New York, Simon and Schuster, 1963.

Chapter XVII

HOW TO MAKE THE INFORMATION WORK FOR YOU

Y OUR adult self has developed from a multitude of conditions arising out of heredity, parental attitudes and behavior, and influences from the society in which you live. The sibling role you had in childhood was only one of the factors which affected your development. It may be, however, of relatively great importance because you lived that role during your most formative years, a rather long period of time, and escaped it not at all during that time.

Your role as a sibling or an only child was a social one; it had to to do with the way other people related to you and with the way you related to other people. Hence we should not expect to find that it had a great deal to do with some of your basic qualities of personality or character. Whether you are moral or anti-social, tolerant or intolerant, kind or vicious—such characteristics are likely to have been learned from your parents or acquired from the societal environment in which you grew up.

It does seem that each position in the family hierarchy, according to birth order, places particular pressures on the child holding that position, and these pressures may encourage the development of certain relative degrees of personality characteristics. These trends have been described in the chapters covering each position in the order of birth.

The greatest impact of your sibling role is likely to be on aspects of your behavior which have to do with relationships with other people.

The adult human being is required by relationships with other people to:

1. Assume certain attitudes toward other people. You will, in general, feel competitive with others, envious or jealous of them,

tolerant and accepting of their needs depending somewhat upon your position in the childhood family hierarchy.

2. Expect to take a certain role in relation to other people. Whether you expect to take charge of situations or to let others take charge, whether you feel yourself to be responsible for getting things done or whether you sit back and allow others to assume responsibility—such assumptions of role will depend to a great extent upon your birth order in your childhood family.

3. React in certain ways toward authority as represented by less intimate relationships outside the home. Your particular sibling position may have a great deal to do with whether or not you can accept supervision comfortably, whether or not you try to move into a position of authority, and how you yourself perform as authority and supervisor.

4. Interact with peers in relationships that are as intimate as your childhood relations with your brothers and sisters. Such peers include close friends and your spouse. These intimate relationships are those which are most likely to call into full play the attitudes and behavior you displayed in relating to your siblings in childhood.

5. To act as a parent with your children. In this relationship you are likely to utilize what you learned of parental attitudes and behavior from your own parents. Since your parents varied their procedures with each child according to his birth order, your own parental attitude will reflect your position in the childhood family.

Much of what you learned in your sibling role forms a constructive part of your personality. The frequent charm of the grown-up only child, the conscientiousness of the oldest child, the adjustability of the middle child, the optimism of the youngest child—these are among the constructive aspects of the adult siblings' personalities.

The sibling role does a great deal more for the individual than make problems for him. We are only concerned with the problems it can make when they get in the way of effective adult adjustment to current realities.

The information in this book can be used not only to increase your understanding of yourself and other people, but it can be used as a basis for changing those aspects of your behavior which may stem out of those old sibling relationships and are only of negative value in meeting the present requirements of your adult life.

Here are some steps that you might take in making the information about sibling role work toward your advantage:

I. Get clearly in mind the tendencies you may have as the result of having been raised in a certain sibling position. You may want to re-read the chapters relating to your childhood role.

II. Select from your experiences the past several days some situation in which you displayed highly adequate ability in relating to other people or in solving some personal problem.

Now study your behavior in that situation. Can you describe to yourself how that behavior might have stemmed out of your sibling position?

For instance, let's say that you are a construction engineer. You were called into a conference in the Chief's office yesterday to go over plans for a new highway bridge. You had some very good ideas. You presented them well and you got the feeling that the Chief was going to ask you to lead the unit that would develop the final plans. It would mean a step up in status and probably in salary.

How does your sibling role fit in? You were oldest child in a family of three children. Was that one reason you were so well able to verbalize your ideas? Was that why you so easily took over as something of a leader in that situation? You felt comfortable about telling others how things were to be done. Perhaps the Chief recognized in you some of the conscientiousness and willingness to accept responsibility that might have developed out of your position as oldest child.

The effective individual usually is able to integrate into his adult behavior aspects of his sibling role that will work for him as an adult. In work situations the skills of the individual usually determine his accomplishments, and both his particular aptitudes and his interests will have an important part in determining the specific occupation he will select in adulthood. The sibling role probably has relatively little to do either with his occupational choice or with his success in that occupation. It is when his occupational function causes him to interact with other people that he will utilize attitudes and behavior learned in the family position in childhood.

Let us take an example of a situation involving close relationships. Your oldest son, aged seventeen, came home last night and reported that he had been in a small accident with your car. You recognized your son's concern and anxiety and you gave him a chance to explain. It did not seem to you that he was at fault and when you went out with him to look at the car, you saw that the damage was limited. You suggested to him that he might even be able to pound out those few dents himself. As you left, he said, "Gee, thanks, Dad, for not getting mad."

Could it be that your sibling role as a middle child in a family of four made it possible for you to view the situation realistically and to control your emotional reactions to it? It might even occur to you that both your father and your oldest brother would have been quick to develop anger and either of them would have thought first of some way to punish the boy.

Another example. Your husband was exhausted last night when he came home from the office. He said he'd been looking forward all afternoon to a cocktail, dinner, and early to bed. You had been tired, too, that day and what you had in mind was a cocktail and dinner, but in a quiet little restaurant rather than at home. But your husband did look unusually tired, so you said, "I don't have much of a dinner in mind and it'll soon be ready. Go fix a martini and while you're about it, fix one for me. We'll have dinner in front of the fire." After two cocktails and dinner, your husband had said, "You're the greatest. I love you, Honey, Let's go to bed."

Why were you able to put his needs first? Why did you feel it so important to "mother" your husband, to indulge him rather than yourself? Could part of the reason be that you had been the older sister of a brother whom you had "mothered" when you were both children? Or were you being adaptable because you were a middle child in your family?

III. Examine some situation in which you were placed the last day or two in which you didn't react as you would have liked.

Ladies first this time: You have just moved into a new neighborhood. Yesterday a neighbor called and suggested that you join her and several other neighborhood women for coffee. You immediately felt uncomfortable about going to the home of someone you had spoken to only casually and you wondered if you would really care to become intimate with neighbors. You gave an excuse for not joining them. Now you wonder why you acted that way. After all, even if you don't want to be friendly, your children want to make friends with the other children in this new neighborhood and they would do so sooner if you became acquainted with the other mothers.

Could the fact that you were raised as an only child have something to do with your reluctance to join a group of ladies you don't know? With your preference to keep your distance until you're more sure of the persons involved?

Apparently your childhood role was causing you to act in an unrealistic and maladaptive way.

Another example: You are a businessman who has a large number of employees. Yesterday you walked unexpectedly into one of the salesrooms and you found three of your salesmen deep in conversation with each other. There were no customers in the room, but you thought that Tom, Dick, and Harry might have been using that time to striaghten the merchandise on the shelves, and you abruptly told them so. Afterwards you regretted your abruptness. After all their sales' records are the best in the store and Harry had recently had a very good offer to work for a competitive firm.

Is it possible that your childhood position as oldest son of seven children developed in you a tendency to be overly authoritarian and to allow neither yourself nor others to take time for relaxation?

IV. Decide upon some one problem that you want to solve within the next day or two. Decide how you are to approach the matter. Are you likely to be adversely affected in your behavior by tendencies that grow out of your childhood sibling role?

Let's say, for instance, that you want to approach your supervisor about a salary increase or about a position with better opportunities for advancement. You decide that you will talk first to his secretary and see if she will convey your request. But, wait a minute! Are you afraid of authority because you were the younger of two boys? Are you resisting the need for aggressive action? Consider how you can adjust your behavior so that it is the behavior of an adult with respect for his own ability who needs to approach, not an older brother nor his father, but another adult who is as interested as you are in utilizing your abilities best in terms of the company's needs.

V. For the next week or two be especially aware as you go about your activities of ways in which your sibling role might be affecting your relationships with other people. Practice reacting to situations in the most realistic and objective way that you can.

By the time you have finished this last step you should have developed the ability to recognize easily the behavior that stems out of your sibling role. You should know the tendencies which influence you to behave as though you are still in the childhood situation, and you will see that they may not be effective in terms of adult requirements. You will be in a position to adjust your behavior to your current reality, and you will be on your way toward a higher level of effective living.

AUTHOR INDEX